More Praise for **BETTER, NOT PERFECT**

"Take some of the best ideas in philosophy, mix in relevant research in psychology, add a lifetime of practical wisdom, and you have a recipe for exactly what this book's subtitle says it is: a realistic guide to doing the most good you can. Read it, and you will find yourself leading a better life—better for you and better for the world!"

—Peter Singer, Princeton University,
author of *Animal Liberation* and *Practical Ethics*

"William James, the great American philosopher who gave us pragmatism, wrote that 'thinking is for doing.' Bazerman's *Better, Not Perfect*, is a perfect exposition of that original ideal brought to bear on twenty-first-century issues. Bazerman has a gift: to grasp the core of the hardest ethical issues we confront, and to bring the best science and arguments to allow us to grapple with them. He does this with such clarity and compassion for human nature that you will be more than persuaded—you'll get up and do something! Max Bazerman is an inspirator who will be your guide in an uncertain world full of promise, if only we make better, not perfect, choices."

—Mahzarin R. Banaji, Harvard University, and coauthor of *Blindspot*

"The world is fraught with crises related to global health, the environment, animal welfare, and more. Nothing is more important than figuring out what we can do to improve things. In *Better, Not Perfect*, Harvard Business School professor Max Bazerman offers a roadmap that will help readers understand the world around them and how they can most strategically and effectively make things better. I spent my first ten years out of college trying to be perfect, not better. Oh, how I wish I'd had this book to guide my vocational decisions."

—Bruce Friedrich, cofounder and executive
director, The Good Food Institute

"Building on the ideas of effective altruism, Bazerman delivers important new insights on how to use your time, money, intellect, and influence to make the world better. *Better, Not Perfect* can help you do an enormous amount of good."

—Will MacAskill, cofounder, Centre for Effective Altruism, and author of *Doing Good Better*

"We all want to believe that we will help make the world a better place. But how do you get to that North Star of doing the most good over your lifetime? Take one step at a time. In his delightful and engaging book, Max Bazerman brings philosophy into our everyday lives and gets us thinking about how to improve our real-life decisions to create more value for our friends, our community, and ultimately our society. Maybe you can reduce meat consumption rather than switch to vegetarianism; maybe you can invent a plant-based meat substitute rather than donating 50 percent of your income to charity. Bazerman calls upon us to be more altruistic—better, but not perfect! More rational thinking and less intuition will help us make better ethical decisions that lead us toward that North Star."

—Sheryl WuDunn, coauthor of *Tightrope*

"Although we're quick to recognize the moral mistakes other people make, it's not until it's too late that we catch most of our own. As a leading expert on this problem, Max Bazerman shows how we can avoid ethical blunders—and do more good along the way."

—Adam Grant, bestselling author of *Give and Take* and *Originals* and host of the TED podcast *WorkLife*

"Max Bazerman is part behavioral scientist, part mensch—and the sage I consult whenever I'm stuck on a life decision. This brilliant, wise guide shows us why perfect really is the enemy of the good— and how we can all do better."

—Angela Duckworth, University of Pennsylvania, bestselling author of *Grit*

BETTER, NOT PERFECT

BETTER, NOT PERFECT

A REALIST'S GUIDE TO MAXIMUM SUSTAINABLE GOODNESS

MAX H. BAZERMAN

HARPER
BUSINESS
An Imprint of HarperCollins*Publishers*

170
BAZ

FIRST EDITION

Library of Congress Cataloging-in-Publication Data
Names: Bazerman, Max H., author.
Title: Better, not perfect : a realist's guide to maximum sustainable goodness / Max H. Bazerman.
Identifiers: LCCN 2019057443 (print) | LCCN 2019057444 (ebook) | ISBN 9780063002708 (hardcover) | ISBN 9780063002715 (ebook)
Subjects: LCSH: Business ethics | Social responsibility of business. | Decision making.
Classification: LCC HF5387 .B388 2020 (print) | LCC HF5387 (ebook) | DDC 174/.4—dc23

20 21 22 23 24 LSC 10 9 8 7 6 5 4 3 2 1

Dedicated to the amazing characters
described in this book who have been core
to showing me the path to be better:

Rachel Atcheson

Becca Bazerdog

Mark Budolfson

Dolly Chugh

Marla Felcher

Bruce Friedrich

Josh Greene

Will MacAskill

Doug Medin

Peter Singer

CONTENTS

PREFACE

In 1993, when I was on the faculty of Northwestern University, I gave a talk at a conference on behavioral science and the environment at the Allen Center, a rather nondescript modern building in Evanston, Illinois, marked by its expansive views of Lake Michigan. In passing, I mentioned that I had become a vegetarian. Someone in the audience made a comment in which he referred to himself as a vegetarian, too, but one who ate fish. I responded, "That would make you a fisheterian." I knew the word "pescatarian," but I was making a very bad attempt at humor. After the talk, the cognitive psychologist Doug Medin approached me. Before I tell you what he said, it's important to know that Doug is a friend of mine who's very mild-mannered, nice, and brilliant. "Max," Doug said, "your combative comment to the guy who ate fish was really stupid." "Stupid" stood out, coming from Doug, but it was accurate. Doug went on to argue, convincingly, that allowing the fish eater to claim vegetarianism would make him less likely to become a red-meat eater and even, in time, more likely to stop eating fish. His point was that each positive step a person takes should be encouraged, rather than highlighted for what it lacks.

I knew Doug was right. With my snarky remark, I had been trying to get the commenter to be more ethical—a poor strategy from lots of perspectives. First, I was trying to impose my goals on another person by suggesting that his ethical behavior was in need of improvement. I was also applying my own value system—particularly, the notion that fish eating is morally wrong—to encourage him to question his fish consumption. In addition, I was failing to think like a social scientist about what would actually lead another person, one I didn't know well, to change his behavior. I am confident that my effort flopped and that Doug understood the psychology of changing the commenter's ethical behavior better than I did.

Over the last few decades, I haven't given up on trying to be more ethical and insightful myself or on encouraging others to be more ethical, but I think I'm going about it in a more effective way. Writing this book has helped me think through how to be more effective at meeting these goals. If I'm successful, this book will make you better—more successful, more ethical, and more effective at creating value for others. We'll explore the latest theories and research findings on what we now know works when it comes to helping people, including ourselves, reach what I call their "maximum sustainable level of goodness."

Of course, to do so, we'll need to reach a shared definition of ethics. I'll depart from utilitarian philosophy, and most philosophies, in that I won't judge the ethicality of your current behavior. Rather, let's assume that all of us would like to create more value for ourselves and others—and that we have more capacity than we realize to be better. I won't expect you to share my values or priorities on issues that have ethical dimensions, such as vegetarianism. I don't want to define a narrow set of societal rules for good behavior. I certainly won't guide you toward adhering to a specific religion. I won't urge you to always tell the truth or to reveal all of your information to your negotiation opponent.

Instead, we'll use the word "ethics" similarly to how utilitarian philosophers use the term: to achieve the greatest good by creating as much value as possible for all sentient beings in the world. By creating more value, you will be better and do better. Our goal will be to identify concrete steps to access our capacity to create more value and reach what I'll refer to as our maximum sustainable level of goodness. That is, the goal won't be to push you toward perfection, but to encourage you on the path of goodness at a level that you can sustain and enjoy for the rest of your life.

WHAT LIES AHEAD

In the first five chapters, we'll explore a new mindset for improving moral decision making that underlies my prescriptive approach (more on that later) to improving ethical behavior. Chapter 1 will expand on my general perspective. We'll see that we all have the potential to create more value for ourselves and society; that we don't need to try to be perfect (we can't be, anyway); and that systematic barriers stand in the way of more ethical behavior. As we'll explore in Chapter 2, activating the full potential of our intelligence is fundamental to making value-maximizing decisions, but cognitive and moral roadblocks sometimes hold us back. By learning effective detours around these roadblocks, we get in the mindset of doing better. Chapter 3 introduces the concept of trade-offs—a familiar topic in the negotiation world—with the goal of creating the most value not only for the parties at the table, but for all. Chapter 4 will make a pitch for avoiding corruption, which sounds pretty obvious, but actually offers far more levers for change than most of us are aware of. Chapter 5 will provide prompts for noticing opportunities to create value that too often escape our attention.

The next four chapters will focus on applying these ideas to areas where most of us can improve: equality/tribalism, reducing waste, using our time better, and making more effective charitable decisions. The final section of the book will offer additional guidance on how to leverage your potential by influencing others to make decisions for the greater good. We will close with some thoughts on how we can achieve our maximum sustainable goodness.

Ethical challenges are not new, but new and different ones are arising every day. Bernard Madoff's theft of billions of dollars reminds us that we are more vulnerable to crooks than ever before—and perhaps more willfully ignorant of their crimes. Terrorism raises tough decisions about what processes are appropriate to get the information that's needed to keep people safe. As companies dream up ever-increasing ways to make our lives easier, our environmental footprint grows deeper and more damaging by the day. In the United States, citizens are challenged on how to act when national leadership no longer shows a preference for truth. In many countries, finding collective value has disappeared as a national goal. We urgently need to find and follow a North Star that creates more ethicality and more value, and that supports us in simply doing *better*.

PART I

A New Mindset for Improving Moral Decision Making

———

CHAPTER 1

BETTER, NOT PERFECT

In April 2018, I was scheduled to be interviewed at an Effective Altruism conference at the Massachusetts Institute of Technology, about three miles from my home in Cambridge, Massachusetts.[1] Unable to attend the whole conference, I arrived about an hour before my interview. I entered a large room filled with a few hundred attendees, most of them under the age of thirty, and had the somewhat random, and definitely lucky, opportunity of hearing the speaker before me, Bruce Friedrich. I had not met Bruce before, but his talk rocked my world—personally and academically. A lawyer and the CEO of the Good Food Institute (gfi.org), Bruce introduced me to a new way of thinking about reducing animal suffering. He noted in his talk that the growth of vegetarianism—a commitment to eating no meat or fish—has been very limited. One clear reason for this is that preaching to your friends about the virtues of vegetarianism is not an effective way to change their behavior or maintain your relationships with them. So, what can a vegetarian do to help others also leverage the benefits of lower consumption of animals and improve society (by improving the environment and human health, making our food production more efficient so that we can feed the world's hungry, and reducing the risks of a growing antibiotic crisis)?

Bruce answered this question by introducing a world of entrepreneurs, investors (some amazingly wealthy), and scientists who are working with the Good Food Institute to create and encourage the consumption of new "meats" that taste very similar to meat, without requiring the pain, suffering, or death of any animals. These alternative meats included new plant-based products already on the market (such as Beyond Meat and the Impossible Burger), as well as "cultivated" (also called "clean" or "cell-based") meat that will be grown from the cells of real animals in a lab and produced without the need for more animal deaths. Bruce argued that producing meat alternatives that are tasty, affordable, and readily available in grocery stores and restaurants is a much more fruitful means of reducing animal suffering than preaching about the negative effects of meat consumption. It's a profitable enterprise, too: within a year of Bruce's talk, at its initial public offering, the relatively new company Beyond Meat was worth $3.77 billion. Months later, the company's value soared billions higher.

Many management scholars define leadership as the ability to change the hearts and minds of their followers. But note that Bruce's strategy had little to do with changing people's values and everything to do with motivating them to change their behavior, with little or no sacrifice required. This is just one example of how we can adjust our own behavior—and encourage others to do the same—in ways that will create more net good. We'll explore many more of them in this book.

THE SPACE BETWEEN

I have spent my career as a business school professor. Business schools aim to offer practical research and instruction on how to do things better. I often offer my students prescriptions for how to do better, from making better decisions to negotiating more effectively to being better more broadly. By contrast, ethicists tend to either be philosophers who highlight how they think people *should* behave, or behavioral scientists who describe how people *actually* behave. We will aim to carve out a space between the philosophical and behavioral science approaches where we can prescribe action to be better. First, we need a clear understanding of the foundations on which we are building.

Philosophy's Normative Approach

Scholars from a range of disciplines have written about ethical decision making, but by far the most dominant influence has come from philosophers. For many centuries, philosophers have debated what constitutes moral action, offering alternative *normative* theories of what people *should do.* These normative theories generally differ on whether they argue for the maximization of aggregate good (utilitarianism), the protection of human rights and basic autonomy (deontologists), or the protection of individual freedom (libertarianism). More broadly, moral philosophies differ in the trade-offs they make between creating value versus respecting people's rights and freedoms. However, they share an orientation toward recommending norms of behavior—a "should" focus. That is, philosophical theories tend to have very clear standards for what constitutes moral behavior. I am confident that I fail to achieve the standards of ethical behavior for most moral philosophies (particularly utilitarianism) on a regular basis and that if I attempted to be purely ethical from a philosophical perspective, I would still fail.

Psychology's Descriptive Approach

In recent decades, particularly after the collapse of Enron at the beginning of the millennium, behavioral scientists entered the ethical arena to create the field of behavioral ethics, which documents how people behave—that is, it offers *descriptive* accounts of what we *actually do*.[2] For example, psychologists have documented how we engage in unethical acts based on our self-interest, without being aware that we're doing so. People think they contribute more than they actually do, and see their organization and those close to them as more worthy than reality dictates. More broadly, behavioral ethics identifies how our surroundings and our psychological processes cause us to engage in ethically questionable behavior that is inconsistent with our own values and preferences. The focus on descriptive research has not been on the truly bad guys that we read about in the newspaper (such as Madoff, Skilling, or Epstein), but on research evidence showing that most good people do some bad things on a pretty regular basis.[3]

Better: Toward a Prescriptive Approach

We'll depart from both philosophy and psychology to chart a course that is *prescriptive*. We can do better than the real-world, intuition-based behavior observed and described by behavioral scientists, without requiring ourselves or others to achieve the unreasonably high standards demanded by utilitarian philosophers. We will go beyond diagnosing what is ethical from a philosophical perspective and where we go wrong from a psychological perspective to finding ways to be more ethical and do more good, given our own preferences. Rather than focusing on what a purely ethical decision would be, we can change our day-to-day decisions and behavior to ensure they add up to a more rewarding life. As we move toward being better, we'll lean on both philosophy and psychology for insights. A carefully orchestrated mix of the two yields a down-to-earth, practical approach to help us do more good with our limited time on this planet, while offering insight into how to be more satisfied with our life's accomplishments in the process. Philosophy will provide us with a goal state; psychology will help us understand why we remain so far from it. By navigating the space between, we can each be better in the world we actually inhabit.

ROAD MAPS FROM OTHER FIELDS

Using normative and descriptive accounts to generate a new prescriptive approach aimed at improving decisions and behavior is novel in the realm of ethics, but we've seen this evolution play out in other fields, namely negotiation and decision making.

Better Negotiations

For decades, research and theory in the field of negotiation was divided into two parts: normative (how people *should* behave) and descriptive (how people *actually* behave). Game theorists from the world of economics offered a normative account of how humans should behave in a world where all parties were completely rational and had the ability to anticipate full rationality in others. In contrast, behavioral scientists offered descriptive accounts of how people actually behave in real life. These two worlds had little interaction. Then Harvard professor Howard Raiffa came along with a brilliant (but terribly titled) concept that merged the two: an asymmetrically prescriptive/descriptive approach to negotiation.[4] Raiffa's core insight was to offer the best advice possible to negotiators, without assuming that their counterparts would act completely rationally. Stanford professor Margaret Neale and I, along with a cohort of excellent colleagues, went on to augment Raiffa's prescriptions by describing how negotiators who are trying to behave more rationally can better anticipate the behavior of the other less-than-fully-rational parties.[5] By adopting the goal of helping negotiators make the very best possible decisions, but accepting more accurate descriptions of how people behave, Raiffa, Neale, myself, and our colleagues were able to pave a useful path that has changed how negotiation is taught at universities and practiced the world over.

Better Decisions

A similar breakthrough occurred in the field of decision making. Until the start of the new millennium, economists studying decision making offered a normative account of how rational actors should behave, while the emerging area of behavioral decision research described people's actual behavior. Implicit in the work of behavioral decision researchers was the assumption that if we can figure out what people do wrong and tell them, we can "debias" their judgment and prompt them to make better decisions. Unfortunately, this assumption turned out to be wrong; research has shown time and again that we do not know how to debias human intuition.[6] For example, no matter how many times people are shown the tendency to be overconfident, they continue to make overconfident choices.[7]

Luckily, we have managed to develop approaches that help people make better decisions *despite* their biases. To take one example, the distinction between System 1 and System 2 cognitive functioning, beautifully illuminated in Daniel Kahneman's book *Thinking, Fast and Slow*, presents a useful distinction between the two main modes of human decision making.[8] System 1 refers to our intuitive system, which is typically fast, automatic, effortless, implicit, and emotional. We make most decisions in life using System 1 thinking—which brand of bread to buy at the supermarket, when to hit the brakes while driving, what to say to someone we've just met. In contrast, System 2 refers to reasoning that is slower, conscious, effortful, explicit, and logical, such as when we think about costs and benefits, use a formula, or talk to some smart friends. Lots of evidence supports the conclusion that System 2, on average, leads to wiser and more moral ethical decisions than System 1. While System 2 doesn't guarantee wise decisions, showing people the benefits of moving from System 1 to System 2 when making important decisions, and encouraging them to do so, moves us in the direction of better, more ethical decisions.[9]

Another prescriptive approach to decision making came from Richard Thaler and Cass Sunstein's influential 2008 book, *Nudge*.[10] While we do not know how to fix people's intuition, Thaler and Sunstein argued that we can redesign the decision-making environment so that wiser decisions will result by anticipating when gut instincts might cause a problem—an intervention strategy known as choice architecture. For example, to address the problem of people undersaving for retirement, many employers now enroll employees automatically in 401(k) programs and allow them to opt out of the plan. Changing the decision-making default from requiring people to enroll to automatic enrollment has been shown to dramatically improve savings rates.

These fruitful developments in the fields of negotiation and decision making offer a road map, borrowing the idea of identifying a useful goal from the normative tool kit (such as making more rational decisions), and combining it with descriptive research that clarifies the limits to optimal behavior. This prescriptive perspective has the potential to transform the way we think about what's right, just, and moral, which will lead us to be better.

A NORTH STAR FOR ETHICS

Our journey seeks to identify what better decisions would look like and chart a path to lead us in that direction. Much of moral philosophy is built on arguments that stipulate what would constitute the most moral behavior in various ethical dilemmas. Through the use of these hypotheticals, philosophers stake out general rules that they believe people should follow when making decisions that have an ethical component.

The most commonly used dilemma to highlight different views of moral behavior is known as the "trolley problem." In the classic form of the problem, you're asked to imagine that you are watching a runaway trolley that is bounding down a track. If you fail to intervene, the trolley will kill five people. You have the power to save these people by hitting a switch that will turn the trolley onto a side track, where it will run over and kill one workman instead. Setting aside potential legal concerns, would it be moral for you to turn the trolley by hitting the switch?[11]

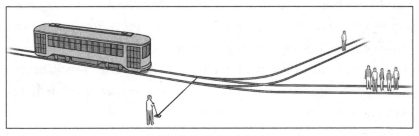

THE TROLLEY PROBLEM

Most people say yes, since the death of five people is obviously worse than the death of one person.[12] In this problem, the popular choice corresponds to utilitarian logic. Utilitarianism, a philosophy rooted in work of scholars such as Jeremy Bentham, John

Stuart Mill, Henry Sidgwick, Peter Singer, and Joshua Greene, argues that moral action should be based on what will maximize utility in the world. This translates into what will create the most value across all sentient beings. Of course, it is very difficult to assess which action will maximize utility across people. But for utilitarians, having this goal in mind provides clarity in lots of decisions—including the trolley problem.

For now, we use utilitarianism as a clear touchstone to help us navigate new terrain. Interestingly, many of us already endorse many of the basic moral constructs of utilitarianism:

- Creating as much value as possible across all sentient beings
- Behaving efficiently in the pursuit of the good that we can create
- Making moral decisions independent of our own wealth or status in society
- Valuing the interests of all equally

Most of my advice will hold up to criticisms of utilitarianism and be relevant even to readers who reject certain aspects of utilitarianism.

For practical purposes, maximizing aggregate value creation across all sentient beings will be the North Star of ethical behavior that we aim for in this book. Yet our behavior is not even close to alignment with these goals. Turning back to psychology, Herbert Simon noted that we have "bounded rationality."[13] That is, while we try to be rational, we face cognitive limitations to our ability to get there. Similarly, we are bounded in our ability to maximize utility in the world, as systematic cognitive barriers keep us from behaving in a more utilitarian fashion. In the chapters to come, we'll explore those barriers and ways to get around them. Some of them are the same as those that keep us from being more rational, and greater self-awareness seeds change. Others require interventions to guard against our ethical blind spots. Either way, if you can do more good at no cost to yourself, it should be easy to move in that direction.

CLEARING SOME HURDLES

Before moving forward with utilitarianism as a North Star, it is useful to consider some of the baggage that comes along with this perspective. First, although many people agree with most, if not all, of the core components of utilitarianism, the term "utilitarianism" often angers people. Utilitarianism is hindered by a terrible name: the word suggests a singular focus on efficiency, selfishness, or even a disdain for humanism—all of which are entirely inconsistent with the intent of the creators. Clearly, Bentham and Mill didn't have a very good marketing department. More recently, Josh Greene has advocated for replacing the term "utilitarianism" with "deep pragmatism." "When your date says, 'I'm a utilitarian,' it's time to ask for the check," he writes in his book *Moral Tribes*. "But, a 'deep pragmatist' you can take home for the night and, later, to meet the parents."[14]

Second, many people ask: Is striving for the greatest good even the right goal? Holding all else equal, virtually all of us want to do more good in the world. But all else *isn't* equal, and the rights, freedom, and autonomy of other people matter to many, as a companion problem to the trolley problem illustrates.

In the footbridge dilemma, the runaway trolley is once again headed down the track and, if ignored, will kill five people. This time, however, you are standing on a bridge above the tracks next to a railway worker who is wearing a large backpack. You can save the five people by pushing the man (and his heavy backpack) off the bridge and onto the tracks below. He will die, but his body will serve as a trolley stopper to save the five. You cannot save the people yourself because you lack the trolley-stopping heavy backpack. Would it be moral for you to save the five people by pushing this stranger to his death?[15]

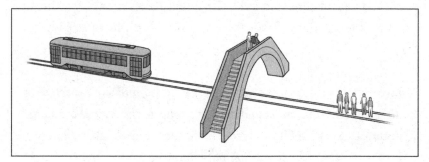

THE FOOTBRIDGE DILEMMA

Most people argue against pushing the man, although the same five-for-one deal is being offered as in the trolley problem. The footbridge dilemma invokes a very different form of morality. When asked why they wouldn't push the man, people tend to say things like, "That would be murder!" "The ends don't justify the means!" or "People have rights!"[16] These are common arguments of deontological philosophers. Thanks to the amazing work of Joshua Greene and his colleagues, we know that our divergent answers to these two problems reflect competing responses in different parts of the brain.[17] In the footbridge problem, when we think about the rights of the potential "victim" being pushed to save five other people, our emotional response activates the ventromedial prefrontal cortex. But when some people override this emotional impulse and create value by saving the most lives possible, the decision is driven by controlled cognitive processes in the dorso-lateral prefrontal cortex.[18] The evidence strongly suggests that the act of pushing the person off the bridge invokes an emotional process that is missing in most of us when we confront the trolley dilemma. Even so, some people make consistent decisions across the two problems: they say they would hit the switch in the first problem and push the man in the second.

But there's one more problem in this series, and this one pushes even avowed utilitarians over the edge, so to speak. It's the surgeon problem, adapted from the late British philosopher Philippa Foot:[19]

Five patients are being cared for at a hospital and are expected to die soon. A sixth man is undergoing a routine checkup at the same hospital. A transplant surgeon in residence finds that the only means of saving the five ailing patients would be to slay the sixth person and transplant his healthy organs into the five. Would it be morally right to do so?

Not surprisingly, most people are appalled by this question and quickly reject this five-for-one deal. Just to be clear, I too am staunchly opposed. Why are so many of us willing to hit the switch in the original trolley problem, yet almost no one is in favor of harvesting the five organs from the healthy person in the surgeon problem? Because even strongly leaning utilitarians bring real-world baggage to their decision making. Namely, we realize that society's many rights and rules create second-order value. That is, if an innocent person can be dragged off the street to save five people dying in a hospital, society will break down, and there will be fewer opportunities to create pleasure and minimize pain. Thus, we utilitarians also value rights, freedoms, and autonomy, but we do so because we believe that these attributes create long-term value. Other philosophies reject this indirect path as a reason to value rights, freedoms, and autonomy, insisting that they have intrinsic worth. Deontologists, for example, demand that in order to be ethical, we must value justice as an end in itself. They argue that the morality of an action should be based on whether that action itself is right or wrong, rather than on net consequences. Thus, deontologists believe no one has a right to push the guy off the bridge in the footbridge problem. Libertarians, meanwhile, believe that individuals are entitled to personal freedoms and autonomy, which outweigh the goal of creating the most good possible in the world.

Utilitarianism has been in conflict with deontology, libertarianism, and other ethical perspectives for a very long time. I'm fascinated by these debates within moral philosophy, while maintaining my view that aiming to create as much good as possible is generally a pretty good path, one that can be adjusted for concerns about justice, rights, freedom, and autonomy in specific situations. For our purposes, it's important to note that you can maintain any value you place on justice, rights, autonomy, and freedom, and still find useful strategies here. The decisions recommended by utilitarianism usually align with those of most other philosophies because they share the goal of doing more good and less harm. When theories conflict, it is because of their contrasting views of morality, which I'm not interested in trying to resolve. It's sufficient for our purposes—striving to be better human beings—to argue that many moral values have both intrinsic value *and* long-term benefits. And, if you have any skepticism about utilitarianism, it is sufficient to simplify the perspective of this book as being that when all other things are about equal, we should strive to create as much value as we can.

A third critique of utilitarianism is that fully maximizing utility in the world is a very tough standard against which to measure our moral decisions. Pure utilitarianism would mean valuing your pleasure and pain no more than the pleasure and pain of any other sentient being, as well as valuing the pleasure and pain of others close to you the same as you value the pleasure and pain of strangers, including those in distant lands. For virtually all of us, this is impossible. As a result, many reject the philosophy, throwing out the goal of moving toward this state with the proverbial bathwater.

As we discussed earlier, while decision researchers do not expect people to be fully rational, they use the concept of rationality as a goal state to help identify changes that will lead us toward more rational (but not perfectly rational) decisions. Similarly, utilitarianism can stand as a North Star for guiding ethical decisions—a goal state that we'll never reach, but that can harness our energy for making better decisions. Utilitarianism serves as a useful guidepost for being better, not perfect.

Finally, one more critique of utilitarianism, and much of moral philosophy, is that it is too often based on strange problems that we would never encounter in real life. Yet "Trolleyland" does have parallels in contemporary reality. For instance, when autonomous vehicles take over the road in the not-too-distant future, they can be expected to eliminate most accidents that occur due to driver error, saving millions of lives in the process. Machine learning will help us create safer roads. But unavoidable accidents will continue, and along with them, unavoidable harm. Our cars will face dilemmas, such as whether to save its passenger or five pedestrians, and car companies will need to program vehicles with algorithms that prioritize such harms. Should the autonomous vehicle protect its passengers, pedestrians, older people, younger people (who could lose more years of life than older people), a pregnant woman (does she count as two people?), and so on?

These are real decisions that are currently being debated. Car manufacturers recognize that the owner of an autonomous vehicle is likely to prefer a program that prioritizes her and her family's life over those of pedestrians she doesn't know. In contrast, regulators might require decision rules that protect as many people as possible.

ETHICS ACROSS DOMAINS

I don't know you, but my quick assessment is that you are a very good person in some domains, pretty good in others, and less good in others that you may not confide about to anyone. I can make that prediction without knowing you because you are human, and human behavior is inconsistent. People who are wonderful to their spouse may view deception in negotiation with a client or colleague to be completely acceptable.

Because it's easier to assess the ethicality of famous people than to take a hard look in the mirror, let's consider philanthropist Andrew Carnegie, whose moral inconsistencies journalist Elizabeth Kolbert documented in *The New Yorker*.[20] After amassing a fortune in steel and railroads during the late 1800s, Carnegie gave away $350 million, about 90 percent of his wealth. He endowed the Carnegie Endowment for International Peace, Carnegie Hall, the Carnegie Foundation, the Carnegie Institute of Technology (now part of Carnegie Mellon University), and more than 2,500 libraries. Carnegie also helpfully shared the reasoning behind his philanthropic decision making, including his belief that people should give their money away while they are alive and that more value is created by donating to the broader community than by leaving money to heirs. While effective altruists might quibble with some of Carnegie's philanthropic choices, there is little doubt that his generosity created enormous value for society.

At the same time, this person who created so much value through his philanthropy also destroyed value by engaging in miserly, ineffective, and potentially criminal behavior as a business leader. Carnegie was very tough on his employees. In an attempt to bust the union at his Homestead, Pennsylvania, steel mill, Carnegie authorized his company, Carnegie Steel Company, to institute massive pay cuts. When the union rejected the new contract, management locked out the workers and brought in hundreds of agents from a detective firm to "guard" the facilities. A battle broke out between workers and agents in which sixteen people were killed. In the end, the union was destroyed and many workers lost their jobs. This 1892 cartoon captured the value-creating and value-destroying impulses of Andrew Carnegie.

A modern-day version of this dichotomy can be seen in the actions of the Sackler family. As a result of its philanthropy, this family's name can be found on many important institutions, including the Sackler Gallery in Washington, the Sackler Museum at Harvard, the Sackler Center for Arts Education at the Guggenheim Museum in New York, the Sackler Wing at the Louvre, the north wing of the Metropolitan Museum of Art in New York, and Sackler research institutes at Oxford, Columbia, and many other universities. The family has also endowed numerous professorships and funded medical research.

Many view the same family as the leading culprit behind the opioid epidemic that has devastated American communities in recent years. The Sacklers' family business, Purdue Pharma, launched the prescription painkiller OxyContin in 1996. The family has made many billions by marketing, and arguably overmarketing, the drug. In 2018, opioids were killing more than one hundred Americans a day, according to most estimates. Purdue is often accused of intentionally encouraging opioid addiction to maximize sales and engaging in a wide variety of unethical promotional practices. The Sacklers have also been accused of inappropriately funneling billions out of Purdue Pharma and hiding their fortune in offshore accounts to shield it from victims.[21] When faced with thousands of lawsuits from cities, states, and other entities for their role in the opioid crisis, the Sacklers refused to accept responsibility and threatened to take Purdue Pharma into bankruptcy protection. Although it's tough to quantify, it seems the Sacklers have created far more harm by selling opioids than the benefits they created through their charitable donations.

In his book *Winners Take All*, Anand Giridharadas argues that society too often lets philanthropists off the hook for the value destruction they cause.[22] In fact, he argues that many of society's biggest philanthropists give away their money precisely to distract citizens from noticing the harm they inflict. I find Giridharadas's arguments to be a bit too cynical, yet I think he nicely highlights that we should judge people by the cumulative net value that they create or destroy, rather than giving them credit for an isolated aspect of their behavior. He also makes the important observation that most of us engage in some activities that create value and others that destroy it. Recognizing the multidimensionality of our behavior and caring about the value and harm we create can help us identify where change might be most useful.

Thus, we should think about our decisions as a whole, taking credit for where we do well, but also noticing where adjustments may be worthwhile. Unfortunately, we spend too little time on this latter task. We may need to accept some changes to our behavior to be more generous, making some personal sacrifices for the good of others. But in addition to sacrificing for the good of others, we can create more value by making wiser decisions. We can also create more value by thinking more clearly, negotiating more effectively, noticing and acting on corruption, and being more aware of opportunities to be better.

CHAPTER 2

CULTIVATING ACTIVE INTELLIGENCE

In 2007, psychologist Mahzarin Banaji, a friend and colleague of mine at Harvard, published a fascinating foreword to the book *Beyond Common Sense: Psychological Science in the Courtroom* about "the moral obligation to be intelligent."[1] Banaji's argument, which started as a talk she gave to entering Yale undergraduates, was that the failure to develop one's cognitive potential would be bad not only for the students, but for society as well. Banaji was trying to encourage her audience to feel an obligation to make wiser choices.

When we make poor decisions, we increase our likelihood of getting sick, dying younger, accepting the wrong job, losing a job, getting married to the wrong person, and losing money. Bad decisions also limit our charitable effectiveness, harm the planet, hurt other people (including family members, friends, and colleagues, not to mention others who share the planet with us), and limit the effectiveness of the organizations we care about the most.

When we see the word "intelligence," we tend to think of it as a fairly fixed personal attribute. However, while it's true that people have different levels of intelligence, we have the power to actively engage the best of our intellectual capabilities to make wise decisions and increase the value we can create in our lives. So, what's standing in our way? There are a number of barriers we need to identify to access our "active intelligence"—the wisdom we bring to our decisions, rather than a fixed trait that describes who we are. Our goal should be to develop the tendency to engage our more active deliberative thought processes (most commonly, our System 2 processes) for important decisions that have ethical import. We all tend to use cognitive (System 1) shortcuts that prevent us from making better and more ethical decisions. As we'll see, willpower and knowledge are needed to access the better decision-making processes that exist within us.

OVERCOMING THE BARRIERS TO ACTIVE INTELLIGENCE

The fields of psychology and behavioral economics provide insights into how we can engage our intelligence more fully and improve our ethical behavior. One opportunity involves reducing our biases. After Herbert Simon's Nobel Prize–winning work on bounded rationality, Daniel Kahneman and Amos Tversky pioneered the modern field of behavioral decision research by delineating the systematic and predictable ways in which individuals deviate from rational decision making. Biases that prevent humans from acting as rationally as they would like to include:[2]

- OVERCONFIDENCE: We tend to be overconfident of the infallibility of our judgments when answering moderately to extremely difficult questions.[3]

- FRAMING: Our preferences for risk are affected by how a problem or decision is framed. Specifically, we'll be more risk-averse when what we could gain is highlighted rather than what we could lose.
- ANCHORING: When making estimates, we base them on whatever initial number or value is available and make insufficient adjustments from that anchor.
- THE CONFIRMATION TRAP: We tend to seek information that supports what we already believe to be true and fail to search for evidence that would disconfirm our beliefs.
- HINDSIGHT: After finding out whether or not an event occurred, we tend to overestimate the degree to which we would have predicted that outcome (such as the likelihood of a particular political candidate winning an election).
- THE CURSE OF KNOWLEDGE: When we have expertise or knowledge in a given area, we have difficulty understanding what the problem would look like to those who lack such expertise or knowledge.[4] Thus, teachers often lack empathy for students who lack their knowledge.

Don Moore and I provide a comprehensive list of decision biases in our book, *Judgment in Managerial Decision Making*.[5]

ETHICAL BIASES

Among the dozens of cognitive biases researchers have identified, some are particularly relevant to ethical decision making. These biases keep us from adhering to our own internal, more reflective moral standards—and most of us are unaware of the degree to which these factors bias our decisions and create harm. These ethical biases emanate from our innumeracy, our desire to receive a warm glow from helping others, a need for connectivity, and a focus on our own perspective.

In his bestselling book *Innumeracy*, mathematics professor John Allen Paulos described the mathematical equivalent of illiteracy: being ineffective with numbers rather than words. This ineffectiveness could be due to a lack of skill or a lack of motivation to think through quantitative information. Paralleling research on cognitive biases, Paulos argued that innumeracy affects both people with lesser educational opportunities and people who are educated and knowledgeable.

Systematic biases limit our ability to think clearly about quantitative information. For example, researchers asked individuals in three different groups how much they would hypothetically pay to save 2,000 (the number given to those in the first group), 20,000 (the number given to those in the second group), or 200,000 (the number given to those in the third group) migrating birds from drowning in uncovered oil ponds. A rational analysis would lead us to expect that, assuming we are concerned about the pain and suffering of birds, the value of saving these three different quantities of birds would be reflected in vastly different levels of willingness to contribute. That is, we should be willing to pay much more to save 200,000 birds than 2,000. Instead, the average amount promised by each group was $80, $78, and $88, respectively—virtually the same amount.[6] This type of innumeracy has been described as *scope insensitivity* or *scope neglect*; that is, the *scope* of the altruistic action had little effect on the magnitude of the contribution made to solve a problem.[7] Kahneman and his colleagues argue that participants in this experiment visualized "a single exhausted bird, its feathers soaked in black oil, unable to escape."[8] The emotionality of the image was the dominant motivator to contribute, regardless of whether 2,000, 20,000, or 200,000 birds were at risk.

We glaze over the zeroes in the quantity and make decisions in reaction to emotional images.

In a 2007 study, decision scientists Deborah Small, George Loewenstein, and Paul Slovic gave participants five dollars each to complete questionnaires.[9] Half were asked to read the following text:

Food shortages in Malawi are affecting more than 3 million children. In Zambia, severe rainfall deficits have resulted in a 42% drop in the maize production from 2000. As a result, an estimated 3 million Zambians face hunger. Four million Angolans—one third of the population—have been forced to flee their homes. More than 11 million people in Ethiopia need immediate food assistance.

The other half saw a picture of a small girl with the message:

Her life would be changed for the better as a result of your financial gift. With your support, and the support of other caring sponsors, Save the Children will work with Rokia's family and other members of the community to help feed her, provide her with an education, as well as basic medical care and hygiene education.

Participants in both conditions were asked if they would like to donate some or all of their five dollars. In the first group, 23 percent contributed; twice as many—46 percent—contributed in the second group. According to the "identifiable victim effect," we tend to offer greater aid when presented with a specific, identifiable victim of a problem than when told about a large, vaguely defined group with the same level of need.[10]

Scope neglect and the identifiable victim effect encourage our intuitive innumeracy and lead to poor decision making. In contrast, most of us would endorse the goal of choosing behaviors—such as contributing money or investing our time—where we can do as much good as possible, rather than simply *feeling* like we made a difference.

Why do we do nice things for other people, like that identifiable victim, in the first place? Is it to create value for others or to get credit in some strange informal competition? Most people would like to believe the former is true, yet Daniel Kahneman and his colleagues convincingly explain the phenomenon of scope neglect by arguing that we contribute enough money to receive a *warm glow* from participating in solving a problem rather than thinking about the maximum amount of good we could do.[11]

To take one example, I personally believe that more good comes from making donations to reduce hunger in emerging economies than from making similar donations to major opera houses. (I realize that the Boston Opera might view me as annoying or lacking cultural sophistication for even expressing this view.) But major cultural venues have a significant advantage over famine relief organizations when it comes to raising funds: They print event programs, and sometimes hang plaques on the wall that list donors by donation level. Similarly, universities benefit from the fact that donors enjoy seeing their names on buildings. People care about the recognition they get from their donations, to the extent that they will give less, or not at all, if they are not recognized for giving.

I would hope that many of us would reconsider our need for recognition, but there is little reason to expect this need to fully disappear. As a result, organizations that do the most good should think about how they might provide recognition to donors.

Philosopher Peter Singer opens some of his lectures by asking those in the audience to imagine that on the way to work, they pass a child drowning in a pond.[12] To save the child, they would have to jump in and get their clothes wet and muddy. Do you have an obligation to save the child? he asks. The audience quickly confirms that they do have that obligation. He then points out that there are millions of children living far away from us whose lives could be saved by contributions from us that we would consider to be about as costly as the wet and the mud. However, we pass on these opportunities. Why? Because the children are far away, not directly visible to us, and not personally identifiable. Most of us do not feel connected to those suffering in far and distant places.

Singer's anecdote helps to clarify why we prefer to give to people in our community rather than to people in distant lands, even when more good could be done with the same contribution: we want to feel a direct connection to the good we will cause. This also helps to explain why we heed the appeals of those who speak to us directly without thinking about whether a more worthy organization farther away could do more with our dollars. Yet, when people are asked to think about how much they value feeling connected to donation recipients, they have trouble justifying this preference and are more prone to contribute where they can do the most good. We intuitively seek connections, while our more active intelligence cares more about the actual impact we can have.

Relatedly, in their research, psychologists Nicholas Epley and Eugene Caruso have documented that we have an amazing capacity to think about the thoughts and the emotions of others, but simply fail to activate this capacity unless those people are right in front of us.[13] We can understand the emotional experience of another person directly as we study their face. We are able to think about our partners' preferences with keen accuracy. We are also capable of imagining what life is like for the poorest people in the world, but we typically fail to activate this imagination.

Cognitive psychologist Boaz Keysar has highlighted this failure to think about others, even when we can, with a concept he calls the "illusory transparency of intent."[14] In the days before we used GPS to get where we needed to go, Keysar described the then-common situation of giving directions to a friend on how to find your home. As you may recall, it wasn't unusual for that friend to get lost and have to find a pay phone (remember, this was pre–cell phones) to call for clarification. Why did our smart friend get lost when our directions were so clear? The answer is that we forget to share familiar details that we rely on without thinking, such as the fact that the road forks to the left a few blocks from our house. We are similarly unhelpful when we give coworkers instructions on how to carry out a task that we perform by rote. More broadly, when instructing others, we fail to think about the task from their perspective—that is, we falsely assume that our intent and knowledge are transparent. The illusory transparency of intent overlaps with the curse of knowledge, discussed above.

For another example of the tendency to be self-focused, consider the common social task of gift giving. How can you choose the ideal gift for someone from a value-maximizing perspective? The goal would be for the recipient to get more value from the gift than the cost (in time and/or money) you incurred from the gift. To meet this goal, you might think about how your knowledge allows you to identify products and services that the recipient would value, but might not even know exist. Now think about the times you have moved and all the things that you can't believe you own, and certainly have no interest in packing and moving. What do these items have in common? My own experience is that they tend to be "whimsical," such as silly books, goofy artwork, or other gag gifts—fun to give and fun to receive, but of little value beyond the day they were given. The giver thought about the experience of giving you the gift, but not about the actual long-term value you would receive from the gift. The broader point is that givers can create more value by looking beyond the enjoyment they would receive from the recipient's initial reaction to consider the recipient's long-term experience with the gift.

Providing further evidence of our self-focus, University of California, Berkeley professor Don Moore, author of *Perfectly Confident*, found in his research that people are biased toward assuming they perform worse than average on objectively difficult tasks (for most people, this would include juggling) and better than average on objectively easy tasks (for most people, this would include driving a car).[15] Of course, most people are bad at difficult tasks, and most people are good at easy tasks. But when assessing how we measure up, most of us simply focus on our own skill at a given task rather than on how our performance compares to that of others, even when we have access to that information.

Similarly, abundant research has shown that self-focus leads people to claim more credit for work and other tasks than they deserve. This is true of rich and poor, women and men, and across ethnic groups. In my work with Nick Epley and Eugene Caruso, we asked coauthors to estimate the percentage of the total work they did on a given academic paper. On average, for papers with four authors, they collectively claimed 140 percent of the credit.[16] These people weren't being intentionally selfish. Rather, they focused on the work they did and not on the work of others. In fact, when Nick, Eugene, and I asked authors how much of the work *each author* did on a paper with four authors, they thought more about the others' work, and their own self-serving biases were reduced by half.

ENGAGING OUR ACTIVE INTELLIGENCE

Looking back at the four sources of bias described in the previous section (innumeracy, warm glow and recognition, connectivity,

and self-focus), you'll see they all put you at the center: your intuition over the correct numbers, your identification with the victim,
your sense of recognition, your connection, and your tendency to
focus on yourself. Creating more value in the world requires that
we think beyond ourselves. A good starting point is to consider our
two primary modes of decision making—System 1 and System 2.

Prescriptive models of decision making encourage us to think
rationally, often by prescribing structures to help us. For example,
in our book, *Judgment in Managerial Decision Making*, Don Moore
and I outlined the following steps for choosing the right option
among multiple choices:[17]

1. Define the problem.
2. Identify the relevant criteria.
3. Weight the criteria.
4. Generate alternatives.
5. Rate each alternative on each criterion.
6. Compute the optimal decision.

This list makes sense to most people, yet when you ask them if
they regularly follow steps like these, they say, "Of course not." In
fact, if you methodically went through each of these steps for every
decision you made at the grocery store, you'd be there for hours.
Following these steps makes more sense when we're facing important decisions, but even here, most of us are far from systematic.

As we discussed in Chapter 1, one way to make better decisions
is to move from System 1 thinking to System 2 thinking. But even
when facing important decisions, we are likely to rely on System
1 thinking when we're very busy. The frantic pace of professional
life suggests that very important leaders lean on their System 1
processes.[18] Moreover, bestselling books, including *Blink* by Mal-
colm Gladwell, give people false hope that they can trust their

intuitive System 1 thinking.[19] In fact, there are plenty of reasons to question our intuition, as even the brightest people make judgmental errors on a regular basis.

Moving from System 1 to System 2 thought can take a variety of forms. It can entail explicitly going through a structured decision-making process like the one detailed above. It can mean critically examining the way your intuition is leaning. It could mean waiting until you are not under time pressure or stress, which is when your intuition is most likely to lead you astray. It might mean asking a smart friend, partner, or colleague to help you analyze the problem or turn the decision over to a group. Or it could involve using a calculator, computer, or algorithm, which will bring more logical analysis to the problem.

Turning to the realm of ethics, Josh Greene uses dual-processing research to argue that people have two separate modes of moral reasoning, just as they have two different modes of decision making. We use System 1 reasoning, our intuitive or instinctual responses, to respond to most moral contexts. Greene provides ample evidence that System 2, our more deliberative system, will lead us to decisions that create more value. Greene's work provides guidance on how to move toward making more utilitarian, value-creating judgments. For the sake of efficiency, we can continue to use our faster, intuitive systems for most of our everyday decisions. But when we can carve out the time, we can create more value by using our more deliberative systems to make more important decisions.

ACTIVE INTELLIGENCE ASSISTS

Ask yourself how you currently create value for yourself and for others. Are there ways you might create more? Interestingly, most people haven't sufficiently examined, or audited, their current ethical behaviors. Once you have the motivation to engage your System 2 thinking more often to be better, you will need some tools. Here are three practical strategies you can use to make more ethical decisions.

Joint, Rather than Separate, Evaluation

We often respond emotionally to moral problems. Unfortunately, our emotion-based decisions tend to be different from those we would make in a more rational state of mind. One reason we give our emotions so much weight in our decisions is that we tend to consider options *one at a time.* Substantial evidence documents that when we evaluate one option (such as a product, a potential employee, a job offer, or a possible vacation), System 1 has a powerful influence on our decisions. By contrast, comparing multiple options simultaneously invokes System 2 processing. Consequently, our decisions are more cognitive, less biased, and more utilitarian.

Take the task of weighing job offers. My colleagues and I asked graduating MBA students whether they would accept various job offers from a consulting firm when facing a deadline.[20] Those in Condition A were told they would receive a moderate salary, the same offered to all graduating MBA students. Those in Condition B were offered a higher salary but learned that some other graduating students were being offered even more. Job A paid less than Job B, but Job B evoked an emotional reaction in students because it raised the moral issue of the firm paying others more than them. Such social comparisons have a strong impact on our judgments and decisions.

Social comparisons and the emotions they trigger have a far greater effect when we're evaluating a single option than when we're comparing two or more options at the same time. When MBA students were offered either Job A or Job B, they rated Job A as more attractive because of their emotional reaction to being offered less than others for Job B. However, when MBA students were asked to imagine that they received *both* offers and had to choose between them, they selected Job B over Job A. The cognition required to engage in joint comparison overrode the MBA students' emotional reactions and allowed them to focus on the fact that Job B would pay them more than Job A.

Would you be interested in a tool that would allow you to hire better people and to discriminate less in the process? In a different study, economists Iris Bohnet, Alexandra van Geen, and I identified joint decision making as such a tool.[21] We determined that when people are evaluating employees one at a time, their System 1 processes tend to dominate. As a result, they tend to rely on gender stereotypes: they lean toward hiring men for mathematical tasks and women for verbal tasks. By comparison, when people are able to compare two or more applicants at a time, they focus more on job-relevant criteria. Their decisions are more ethical toward job candidates, and organizational performance improves.

The Veil of Ignorance

Philosopher John Rawls offered the image of a "veil of ignorance" as a means of thinking through what would be best for society.[22] Rawls's challenge is to imagine that you know nothing about your position in society. In this uninformed state, behind a veil of ignorance, you will be in a better position to decide how society should be structured for the greater good. Rawls intuitively understood that your status, wealth, position, and so on form cognitive barriers to objectively assessing what is just. Under a veil of ignorance, you could do better.

A veil of ignorance that keeps us from knowing our role in many ethical real-life decisions should enable us to make wiser, more moral decisions. Let's return to the last problem we considered in Chapter 1, in which five people are dying in a hospital and a surgeon has the opportunity to kill a healthy person to save them. Imagine that you knew you were one of the six people described in this problem, but had Rawls's veil of ignorance and didn't know which of the six people you were. I predict that you would now be more in favor of saving five people at the expense of one. After all, the death of the healthy person would give you an 83 percent chance of survival instead of a 17 percent chance. This thought process might move your decision in a utilitarian direction, even after you remove yourself from being one of the six key actors in the story. Karen Huang, Josh Greene, and I confirmed this prediction in a series of experimental studies.[23]

Rawls thought about the problem of how to help us ignore who we are. Another strategy that can improve our ethicality and objectivity is to intentionally be unaware of who *other* people are, so that we aren't biased by their demographic information. Consider that in the 1960s, less than 10 percent of musicians in the major U.S. orchestras were female. This has changed dramatically, thanks in part to a simple change orchestras have made to their audition process: the addition of a screen between the musician and judges. In the past, judges watched musicians as they auditioned. Now, it's the norm for musicians to perform behind a screen, which forces judges to evaluate what they hear rather than being distracted by what they see—and by their stereotypes of what constitutes a professional musician.[24] Similarly, tech firms are increasingly eliminating names and pictures from the first round of job screenings to gain the ethical and objective benefits of blinding judges from the people they are considering.

More practically, I encourage you to try taking your identity out of the decision-making process. For instance, when considering candidates for a new position with your organization, try to ignore your power, your religion, where you went to school, and other traits. Or, in thinking about what a fair tax system would look like, imagine that you were born into your country with a random level of wealth. Without knowing what your wealth would be, what taxation structure would be fair? By adopting a veil of ignorance, we reduce our self-serving biases, and we enhance the morality of our decisions.

Pre-commitment

It is not always possible to adopt a veil of ignorance or to compare multiple people at the same time when making decisions with an ethical component. Another useful strategy may be to pre-commit to your goals before you are in the midst of making a specific decision. Let's suppose you want to hire someone for a job requiring quantitative skills. Due to the constraints of the situation, you need to search until you find a good candidate and then try to hire them; that is, you need to consider one candidate at a time. How can you make a decision that will not be sexist and that will lead you to hire the best candidate for your organization?

In collaboration with Linda Chang, Mina Cikara, and Iris Bohnet, I have found that decision makers who first think through the criteria they are seeking in a new employee before considering a specific candidate make less sexist decisions and tend to hire a better-quality employee.[25] When we think about our hiring criteria in advance, we engage in System 2 thinking about what would constitute a good choice. In contrast, when we consider a specific candidate without such pre-commitment, our System 1 processes are likely to prevail, including many of the biases that reduce the quality and morality of our decisions.

Joint decision making, imposing a veil of ignorance, and pre-commitment all move us from System 1 thinking toward System 2 thinking—and toward better, more moral decisions. Speaking more broadly, we can all more actively engage our intellect and make better, more moral decisions as a result. In the next chapter, we will confront a critical cognitive barrier that arises when we're making decisions that involve other people—our tendency to see the size of the pie as fixed. When we move beyond the myth of assuming that what's best for us is incompatible with doing the right thing, a path opens up to the ethically efficient frontier where both are possible.

CHAPTER 3

MAKING WISE TRADE-OFFS

What is more important, your salary or the type of work you perform? The quality of the wine or the taste of the food? The location of a house that's for sale or its size? Saving money or enjoying life day by day?

Weirdly, my experience is that most people will readily provide answers to such comparisons despite not knowing how much salary they'd have to sacrifice to get more job enjoyment or how much better the location of the house is as compared to its change in size. Decision analysts tell us that we shouldn't answer these questions based simply on which attribute *feels* most important to us. Rather, we need to know how much of one attribute we are giving up to gain on the other.

It's common for politicians running for office to promise to do everything possible to make sure that "your taxes will go down," "you can have the doctor of your choice," "the government will protect the natural environment," "we will have the strongest armed forces possible," "the national debt will not grow," and so on. Voters like these simplistic promises—at least, they like the ones that are consistent with their politics. But wise leaders realize that there are trade-offs involved: if you grow the military, spend more on social services, and reduce taxes, the national debt is bound to increase. And often, the trade-offs that would be required to fulfill a promise just don't make sense. On many trades, we would gain very little on one dimension while incurring great cost on other dimensions. We also overlook many trades that would create value and have broad support, such as making it easier for citizens to vote.

To pick the right job, house, or vacation, or to make a great public policy decision, we need to make wise trade-offs across various dimensions. When you make wise trade-offs, you are trading up and creating value. Some decisions are easy because the trade-off is obvious. If you're choosing between a job that you think would be challenging and fun, and one that sounds boring but would pay $1,000 more per year, it may be easy to choose the more interesting job. Tougher decisions pit one criterion against another, and the options feel similar in overall value. If the less interesting of the two jobs would pay $20,000 more per year, and you still have a bunch of college debt, for example, the decision may feel much harder because the jobs each excel on different criteria. Too often, people rely only on their intuition to make such decisions and overweight emotional criteria as a result. That is why it may well be useful to compare the choices more methodically. You might create two columns with the two options at the top, then list the criteria on the left-hand side and assess how important each criterion is to you, as well as how each option does on each of the criteria. Sounds a bit formal, but allowing your System 2 thinking to check your System 1 intuition can often help you make smarter trade-offs.

When making our most important decisions, often those with implications beyond ourselves, we'll create more value by making wise trades across a variety of criteria. Consider Charity Navigator, an online platform that provides useful information about the percentage of donated funds that nonprofits use for overhead. Charity Navigator is an extreme proponent of charities maintaining low overhead. I agree that low overhead is a good goal for nonprofits to pursue. But, like those in the effective altruism movement, I believe that other characteristics of charities are also relevant, including their effectiveness, the amount of good they do per charitable dollar, and the integrity and generosity of their leaders. For example, a charity might have a high overhead rate because it spends money on research and competitive salaries to attract and retain the best staff, just like many of the most successful businesses. If this staff can create a more effective organization, the higher overhead might be worthwhile. As an easy-to-use metric, a focus on overhead may prevent organizations from making wise trade-offs against other important criteria, such as their effectiveness or the net amount of value that they create.

In the prior chapter, we overviewed evidence that when we evaluate one option at a time, our intuitive system guides our decision making, we make worse decisions, and we create less value, in comparison to when we compare two or more options. Lucius Caviola and his colleagues use this research to show that we pay more attention to overhead rates when we assess one charity at a time, and focus more on overall effectiveness and make wiser donation decisions when we compare charities.[1] We will return to the realm of philanthropy in much more detail in Chapter 9.

CREATING AND CLAIMING VALUE IN NEGOTIATION

The simplest kinds of trade-offs we can make are limited to our own personal decisions—where to live, which job to take, etc.

When other people have a say in our decisions, we often need to negotiate. In negotiation, the potential for trade-offs is widespread: we face trade-offs between the multiple issues being negotiated, between competing and cooperating with our counterpart, and in making decisions that benefit our own group versus society at large. We create value by trading off issues that are of differential importance to the different parties. These problems have been well analyzed in negotiation and game theory. However, the analysis has focused on what is best for individual decision makers alone. To the extent that you care about others and society at large, your decisions should tilt toward creating value, cooperation, and thinking about ever-broader groups.

Imagine that it is Friday evening, and you and your significant other have agreed to go out but have made no specific plans. If you're like many couples, when you start talking about dinner, your significant other prefers restaurant A, while you prefer restaurant C. Since you are both reasonable people, you compromise on restaurant B. Over dinner, you agree to continue on to a movie. Your significant other proposes movie D, and you counter with movie F. Again, being reasonable people, you compromise on movie E. The B-E combo makes for a fine evening. But on the way home, you both realize that your significant other cared more about the restaurant choice, and the movie choice was much more important to you. As a result, the A-F combo would have been preferable to both of you. The B-E combo failed to create the value that was available from the A-F choice.

This quaint, unimportant example highlights a way of thinking about negotiation—one that focuses on value creation. A very simple principle, taught in virtually any negotiation course, is that you can create value by making trade-offs across issues. This means that any time there are two or more issues in a negotiation (dinner/movie or price/financing terms/timing of delivery), it is critical to learn how important the various issues are to all parties involved so that you can seek trade-offs. Notice that even if you haven't bought into the utilitarian tilt of this book, you would still want to find wise trade-offs in a given negotiation so that you could create a larger pie to divide up with the other side.

The importance of searching for trade-offs in negotiation is shown in the graph below. Based on my many years of teaching negotiation and consulting executives, I can tell you that it is common for parties to settle on deals that resemble Agreement A: the parties have reached agreement, and both are getting value from the agreement, but there are many other agreements available that would provide them with more value. Note that Agreements D, E, and F are all better from both parties' perspectives than Agreement A, but that you would prefer D, and the other party would prefer F. This tension between you and your counterpart

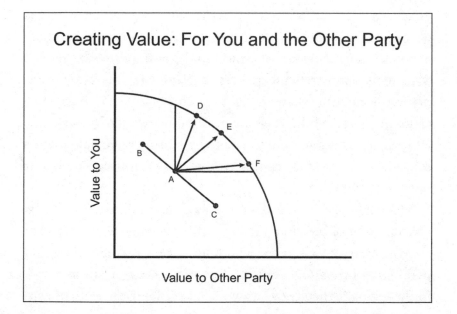

Creating Value: For You and the Other Party

on claiming value often prevents the wise search for value and leaves parties with the pathetic Agreement A instead.

When I teach negotiation, many students enter my course thinking of themselves as great negotiators. What they typically mean by this is that they are good at price haggling and do not keep track of how many deals they have blown by being too tough. Most of these self-described "great negotiators" have rarely thought about value creation. They often suffer from what we call the mythical fixed pie of negotiation. That is, they falsely assume the size of the pie to be carved up is fixed.

Now, many contests are win–lose, including athletic competitions, admissions to private schools, and corporate battles for market share, but in most negotiations, we have the potential to expand the size of the pie. We can do this by making value-creating trade-offs across issues so that both parties get more of what they care about most. We encourage negotiation students to create as much value as possible, or in more technical language, to negotiate along the Pareto-efficient frontier, which is defined as the set of possible agreements that exist such that there is no other agreement that would make both parties better off. Many negotiators remain concerned that if they share the information needed to create value, the other party may be able to claim more value from them, and they don't want to be a sucker. Deepak Malhotra and I explore how you can create value while reducing the risk of losing out on the value-claiming side in our book, *Negotiation Genius.*[2]

Sticking with this typical error of assuming a fixed pie, let's look at a variation of the same graph on the next page. Consider your current state of existence, where you are creating a bunch of good for yourself and a bunch of good for the rest of the world. In the following depiction, we will call your current state of existence "A."

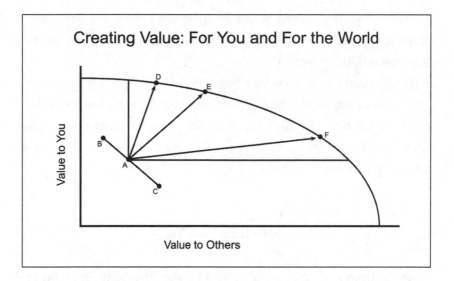

If you became less generous, you'd move from point A toward point B, and if you became more generous, you'd move from Point A to Point C. But what about the less costly and more powerful impact you can make by moving toward Points D, E, and F, where you can get more value for yourself while also creating more value for society? This chapter focuses on how you can do more good, not only by your generosity, but also by your effectiveness in moving to the northeast of this chart in how you make decisions, negotiate, and seek opportunities to find the trades that create value.

Finally, note that the horizontal axis in this representation is longer than the vertical axis (and that line A-F is longer than line A-D). This highlights that the amount of good you can do for others is far larger than the good you can do for yourself with the same level of resources. As utilitarianism highlights, a fixed sum of money is far more useful for the needy than it is for someone well-off enough to be reading this book. For our purposes, and from a utilitarian perspective, suffice it to say that it would be a shame if your concern about moving a bit from Agreement A toward Agreement C kept you from moving dramatically in the direction of Agreement E.

Even if you sometimes lose value, focusing more on value creation works out in the end. What you lose by focusing on value creation will occasionally cost you a bit, but is far more than made up for by the value you can create for others. In the process, you are using one more strategy to make the world better.

ON FREE TRADE

In the summer of 2018, I was asked by the Program on Negotiation at Harvard Law School, "What's the biggest recent mistake you've seen in a negotiation?"[3] The answer was obvious:

> The biggest recent mistake I've seen was . . . the United States government's negotiation with the Chinese government over trade. If you want to confront an economic competitor in a global economy, gaining leverage (by making sure other trading colleagues are on your side) is critical. In this case, the U.S. government alienated many countries prior to the negotiation, losing the power of our allies. The . . . overly simplistic and naively aggressive approach to negotiation just won't cut it in our current global economic environment.

American trade policy in 2018–20 defines the mythical fixed-pie mindset, as it has been based on the assumption that what one side gains, the other loses. By 2016, the United States was recovering nicely from the 2008 recession and was well on its way to reestablishing its economic power. This recovery included a series of international free-trade agreements. Free trade creates value in numerous ways.[4] It promotes efficiency through greater competition. It allows a country to specialize in what it is best at producing and trade with countries that can produce other goods where it lacks a comparative advantage. Due to free trade, consumers benefit from access to a great variety of goods and lower prices through competition. Free trade breaks up single-country monopolies by adding competition from outside that country. Free trade also promotes knowledge transfer and even reduces the likelihood of war, as countries rarely attack significant trading partners. Overall, free trade creates net value for all countries involved in a trade agreement. However, within specific countries, there may be losers as a result—often, industries and unions in areas where another country offers better or cheaper products.

There were multiple reasons for the United States to be unhappy with its trading status with China leading up to 2018. China had a consistent record of requiring foreign companies to enter local joint ventures with Chinese firms in order to enter the Chinese market. Foreign companies also submitted to having their intellectual property "inspected" by the Chinese government, which many U.S. officials view as a convenient way for Chinese entities to steal intellectual property. Many other countries shared such concerns but lacked the power to act on them.

While the trading regime that existed through 2016 may have created net value for both the United States and China, there was a case to be made that the existing set of agreements was closer to Point F in the graphs above and that the United States should force a renegotiation to get to Point E or even Point D. However, the United States falsely assumed a mythical fixed pie, which led the negotiations off the Pareto-efficient frontier, back toward Point A, or worse. Specifically, to try to secure unreciprocated concessions from China, America imposed tariffs on Chinese imports. Instead of concessions, China predictably retaliated with tariffs on U.S. exports to China.

If you want to start a trade war, it is wise to think about what the countries you pick your fight with will do in return. It is predictable that if China loses part of the U.S. market, China will reach out to other trading partners to replace U.S. demand. Interestingly, many of these other trading partners were annoyed with China for the same reasons that the United States was annoyed with China. Thus, any wise negotiator would see the need to coordinate trade strategy with our allies. Unfortunately, America chose to antagonize most key trading partners around the same time. As a result, many other trading partners focused on enhancing their relations with China at the very time that the United States could have benefited from presenting a united front. In the case of this trade war, the pain inflicted on China is far less than that experienced by the United States, and the value creation available through free trade was lost.

MANAGING THE TRADE-OFF BETWEEN COOPERATION AND COMPETITION

The trade war story highlights another puzzle to solve in terms of trade-offs and the global good: the tension between cooperation and competition. Let's switch to some common choices you might confront. Should you help your peers at work succeed in their jobs or compete with them so that you are more likely to get the next promotion? Should you highlight the help you received from others when touting a success or claim the credit for yourself? These are just two examples of the very common trade-off we face between cooperating and competing.

In fact, this trade-off lies at the heart of the most famous game theory problem ever created, one in which you and a "colleague" have been arrested. The police have enough evidence to convict you of a lesser crime and to send you both to jail for a year. However, the police believe (correctly) that the two of you committed a more serious crime. You, Prisoner A, and your colleague, Prisoner B, have been separated and placed in different rooms. The police have offered you a deal:[5]

If you confess and your colleague doesn't, you can turn on your colleague, providing the police with the evidence that they need to convict your colleague. Your colleague will get three years in jail, and you will get no prison time.

Unfortunately for you, the police have offered your colleague the same deal (see the top figure on the next page). They also have clarified that if you both confess, you will each get two years. You and your colleague are facing the same problem: together, you are both better off not confessing (you each get one year) than confessing (you each get two years), yet each of you is individually better off confessing, regardless of what the other party does. That is, if your colleague confesses, confessing results in you getting two years rather than one year, and if your colleague doesn't confess, confessing results in you going free rather than serving one year. Thus, while you are collectively better off cooperating with each other, each of you has an incentive to defect, or compete.[6]

This "prisoner's dilemma" game has become famous because it captures the essence of the trade-off between competing and cooperating. The game has become a prototype used to determine

		Prisoner B	
		Prisoner B stays silent *(cooperates)*	Prisoner B betrays *(defects)*
Prisoner A	Prisoner A stays silent *(cooperates)*	Each serves 1 year	Prisoner A: 3 years Prisoner B: goes free
	Prisoner A betrays *(defects)*	Prisoner A: goes free Prisoner B: 3 years	Each serves 2 years

what factors affect the decision to cooperate and to identify how to think about trade-offs between cooperating and competing when you are not sure what others will do. The prisoner's dilemma has been the subject of thousands of scientific papers. In the process, it has been abstracted to look more like the following problem (it's useful to think of the units as money, such as dollars):

		Player B	
		Cooperate	Defect
Player A	Cooperate	A: 3 B: 3	A: 0 B: 5
	Defect	A: 5 B: 0	A: 1 B: 1

In many of these papers, participants play the game over and over again with the same "colleague," and find out whether the colleague competed or cooperated on each prior trial. Would you cooperate or defect (compete) if you were playing one round of the game? How would your strategy differ if you were playing many rounds? A psychologist by the name of Anatol Rappaport advocated a strategy called "tit-for-tat" for prisoner's dilemma games played a large number of times. This strategy called for a player to cooperate with the other player in Round 1 and then match whatever action the other player took in the prior round, for all subsequent rounds—that is, your colleague's action in Round 1 determines your action in Round 2; your colleague's action in Round 2 determines your action in Round 3, and so on, for as many as two hundred rounds.

Political scientist Robert Axelrod created a fascinating study to find out what strategy is most effective in multi-round prisoner dilemma games. Rather than using college students as participants (as most studies did at the time—this was before the internet existed), Axelrod invited experts on the prisoner dilemma game, namely academic social scientists, to submit their best strategy for a competition to determine which worked best. He told all potential participants in advance that each strategy would be tested against each other strategy in a two-hundred-round version of the game. Each strategy would accumulate points through the tournament and be ranked accordingly. There were fourteen entries, and Rappaport's tit-for-tat strategy won. Axelrod published the results, and at the end of the article, welcomed entries for a second tournament. Once again, tit-for-tat won, this time in a competition with sixty-nine entries. Many additional prisoner's dilemma tournaments have been held, and tit-for-tat, and some minor variations on it, continued to do extremely well.

But tit-for-tat is not the take-home message. Rather, for managing relationships in the real world and creating more value, Axelrod notes that the effective strategies were nice, simple, responsive, and forgiving. Nice strategies start out by aiming to create positive relationships. In iterated games, nice strategies cooperate in Round 1 and continue to cooperate as long as the other party also does. In real life, nice strategies look for the best in others and accept the small risk that not-nice people will take advantage of them. In addition, simple strategies make cooperation easier to understand than competition. Of course, being nice can also lead to being suckered. If you cooperate, and your colleague does not, you get the very worst outcome possible, but you are only suckered for one round. In the prisoner's dilemma tournaments, some of the experts submitted strategies that went to great lengths to gain an advantage over "nice" strategies. They often got short-term gains, but did not succeed over the long term.

A third key to tit-for-tat's success is that it is responsive: it communicates to the other party that they will not get away with competing for long. Finally, tit-for-tat is forgiving. It doesn't hold a grudge. When the other side demonstrates new cooperative behavior, tit-for-tat is open to reestablishing an effective, value-creating relationship. Overdoing punishment can lead conflict to escalate. Tit-for-tat *cannot* score higher than its direct competitor. It can only do "as good as" the party it is playing against in a specific game, since it never competes unprompted. Yet it won the tournaments by consistently developing mutually beneficial relationships. While this book advocates for creating value beyond yourself, I would argue that tit-for-tat is more utilitarian than even the nice strategy of always cooperating, because it helps move the other party toward being more cooperative, which in turn helps create more joint value.

I work in a strange industry—academia. The professionals in this industry generally lay claim to the social missions of creating new knowledge and training the next generation of leaders. On many dimensions, Harvard competes with other fine universities, such as Stanford, Northwestern, and Oxford. We aggressively compete for the best entering undergraduate and MBA students. We compete to sell our executive education offerings. And we compete to be as highly ranked as possible. But one aspect of academia that I find fascinating is the degree to which we radically cooperate on lots of fronts. We share our research with competitive universities as fast as we can. We similarly share our pedagogical insights. Perhaps the most amazing cooperation occurs when one university spends a couple of hundred thousand dollars to train and mentor a Ph.D. student, with the expressed goal of placing that new Ph.D. in a job with one of our main competitors rather than hiring that student ourselves. From the perspective of almost any other industry, this choice of cooperation over competition is bizarre. Yet this norm allows academia as a whole to discover good ideas more effectively and to improve the quality of education across universities. In the process, it allows universities to create more societal value. I have always been proud of our cooperation across different member institutions.

We all experience tensions between cooperation and competition, tensions that involve real trade-offs. We don't like to be suckered by someone who takes advantage of our cooperation. But from a long-term perspective, it is undoubtedly worth suffering the occasional one-time small loss in return for finding many long-term beneficial relationships. The key mistake we make, which leads us away from this insight, is to obsess about being suckered in our current situation when, from a long-term perspective, a life that seeks cooperation at every turn is likely to be far more effective. This is true even before we think about creating value for others. When we do think about and value the outcomes of others, the case for greater cooperation becomes overwhelming.

MAXIMIZING GLOBALLY OR LOCALLY

One common criticism of nonprofit organizations is that there are often too many of them working on the same problem. That is, there are five nonprofits doing the work that one integrated organization could do more effectively; as a result, they miss the opportunity to reduce combined overhead costs that could be used to do more good. We will return to this example when we discuss waste in Chapter 7. The more global concern, and the one I believe gets too little attention, is how this segment of the nonprofit world could be better organized to create as much value as possible for the social cause in question. A wise restructuring of the sector could do a great amount of good.

The key is to see that focusing on what is best for your organization may be at odds with creating the maximal benefit for the organization's actual purpose. But reducing overhead by merging would mean that some organizational leaders would lose their jobs or could no longer be at the top of the organization. In addition, each organization will have strong views on minor topics, and their preferences will not always win out in the merged organization. Thus, while the recipients of the nonprofit organizations may be better off, the myopic needs of specific organizations and their members might be negatively affected. So, what trade-offs should we make between the needs of the current organizations and the recipients of the social services? I hope that the answer is obvious. In the nonprofit world, we should try to create the most good we can with the resources available. This means that

nonprofit leaders should be willing to sacrifice prestige and freedom to create more effective organizations to serve their social
goals. Too often, we fail at making these trade-offs.

This point about cooperation goes well beyond nonprofits. One
of my favorite teaching tools is a decision-making simulation
called Carter Racing, written by Jack Brittain and Sim Sitkin.[7] The
simulation puts participants in the role of owners of a high-level
car racing team. The challenge facing the team is whether or not
to race a race car, when success (placing in the top five) would
create a major win in terms of getting additional funding, when
failure would end the company, and when some members of the
racing team are concerned about racing in the cold weather that is
expected at race time.[8]

When I teach this simulation, executives first make an individual decision of whether to race or not race. I then send them off in
groups of seven to make a group decision. When they come back
to class, I ask them what goal they had as they headed toward the
group meeting. Did they want to:

a) gather insights from the other six members to make the
best decision possible, or

b) get three other members to agree with them so that they
could outvote those in the minority?

Most executives admit to pursuing the latter goal, even as they
recognize that the former goal is the best way to make an in-
formed decision and achieve more effective outcomes.

One of the tasks of an effective leader is to focus all organizational units on meeting a common objective rather than on
winning internal power contests. Focusing on the overall entity
leads to greater effectiveness and moves the organization to the

Pareto-efficient frontier, which ultimately creates value. Thus, while there may be some ambiguity about whether seeking the collectively best solution is best for you in a specific situation, looking for the best overall strategy is a good goal in life and a great way to maximize societal welfare.

We are often presented with the challenge of focusing on a smaller unit (our family, community, city, church, or department) or a broader unit (for example, the organization, rather than just your department). If our goal is to create as much good as possible, then we tend to focus too narrowly. From a utilitarian perspective, moral decisions come from asking what will do the most good rather than what will do the most good for a small group that happens to be closely connected to us.

When you consistently fail to make wise trade-offs between saving and spending money, very bad things can happen—to you. When you focus narrowly on claiming value, beating the competition, and securing a winning coalition, you may or may not do better for yourself in the short term, but there is a good chance you will suffer reputational damage. The failure to cooperate and think more globally will limit your ability to create value for you and the world. Like effective negotiators, those of us who want to achieve our maximum sustainable goodness need to harness the power of finding wise trades.

CHAPTER 4

DISRUPTING CORRUPTION

I generally believe in the power of markets and competition. They aren't perfect, but they are very good at creating value in society. I also appreciate pharmaceutical firms for creating innovations that have allowed us to live longer and healthier lives. In fact, I have proudly provided consulting and teaching services to many of these companies. But I don't like the corrupt practices of pharmaceutical firms that limit the effectiveness of markets, steal value from customers, and destroy overall societal value along the way. We allow this particular type of corruption too often.

Rising health-care costs are a pressing societal problem in the United States, which far outspends any other country on health care. Prescription drugs make up a significant percentage of these costs, about 10 percent in 2017.[1] Extreme drug prices typically occur when a pharmaceutical firm has a monopoly over a particular drug. Generic drugs dramatically reduce costs by breaking these monopolies. But some branded pharmaceutical firms go to great lengths to keep generics out of the market—often by behaving corruptly.

To encourage innovation, governments allow pharmaceutical firms to obtain patents, which encourage them to innovate and disclose those innovations by allowing a temporary monopoly to recoup the investments made during the development period. When drug patents expire, generics can enter the market, at which point drug prices plummet—often by as much as 80 to 90 percent. The government must try to strike a tricky balance between creating an incentive for companies to create new drugs, via longer patent periods and more restrictions on bringing related products to market, and increasing access to drugs for the most vulnerable in society, by allowing generic companies to bring lower-priced drugs to market. To interfere with this cycle and keep their monopoly profits, pharmaceutical firms sometimes indirectly pay generic competitors to stay out of the market. While it is illegal to pay directly, branded firms accomplish this goal by overpaying for "side deals."

The first documented case of a branded pharmaceutical firm paying to keep generic drugs out of the market occurred in 2001 when the Federal Trade Commission (or FTC, which is responsible for preventing the illegal restriction of trade) brought a lawsuit against brand-name drug producer Schering-Plough and generic producer Upsher-Smith.[2] Upsher-Smith had been on the verge of introducing a generic version of K-Dur, a potassium chloride supplement used to correct low potassium in the blood, which was a near-monopoly drug for Schering-Plough. Upsher-Smith argued it could introduce its product to the market without violating Schering-Plough's patent. Schering-Plough sued Upsher-Smith for patent infringement to try to keep it out of the market. Rather than fighting the dispute in court, however, the two companies ended up negotiating. They reached a deal in which Upsher-Smith agreed to wait until very close to the end of Schering-Plough's patent to sell a generic version of K-Dur and, in the very same legal agreement, to accept $60 million from Schering-Plough for five unrelated patents. The FTC sued both companies, arguing that the $60 million wasn't actually for the five unrelated patents but rather was primarily a payment to keep Upsher-Smith out of the K-Dur market and allow Schering-Plough to maintain its monopoly prices.

In response to the FTC's accusations, lawyers for the pharmaceutical firms argued that making trade-offs across issues created value and was therefore beneficial to society. This view was supported by a well-recognized expert in dispute resolution, who highlighted value creation as one of the major contributions of the negotiation literature. This argument follows directly from the logic I presented in Chapter 3: parties who expand the pie by adding issues to the discussion move to the northeast of the negotiation diagram in Chapter 3 and generally create value for the two parties at the table. But, as James Gillespie and I have argued, value-creating deals typically aren't good for society if the value created is shared by only two colluding firms at the expense of their customers, who would end up paying more as a result.[3] When two firms create value by taking it from parties not at the table (those who need the drug), parasitic value creation has occurred.

As an expert witness in the Schering-Plough/Upsher-Smith case, I argued that allowing the firms to collude by combining patent settlement with side deals would create a blueprint that branded pharmaceutical firms with monopolies could follow to pay competitors to stay out of the market. By justifying sham payments, the pharmaceutical firms would skirt the law, with little concern for the harmful effects of their actions on consumers and, more broadly, society.

The administrative law judge hearing the case ruled against the

FTC, largely arguing that it had not produced evidence connecting the market delay to the $60 million payment. The FTC commissioners overruled the administrative judge in a 5–0 ruling, across party lines, based on the observation that these two hostile firms would not have reached the two agreements independently. The pharmaceutical firms, however, won once again on appeal, and the Supreme Court refused to hear the FTC's appeal further. It is my opinion that the administrative law judge provided a publicly available playbook for future parasitic integration among competitors. In the two decades since, many pharmaceutical firms have followed the blueprint provided by the administrative law judge and the appeals court to extend their monopolies on drugs, often with greater deniability and complexity.

The strategy is pretty straightforward: sue any competitor that threatens your monopoly, then settle the case to delay the generic drug's entry into the market and vastly overpay the potential new entrant for some unrelated side deal. After the FTC sued it for reaching this type of deal, brand-name pharmaceutical firm Cephalon agreed to pay a $1.2 billion settlement in 2015. The case was much more complex than the Schering-Plough case, and Cephalon never admitted to violating the law. However, the company's willingness to settle for $1.2 billion—billion, not million—suggests the FTC had solid evidence that the brand-name manufacturer was paying a generic manufacturer to delay market entry. How else to explain such a huge settlement?[4]

Sana Rafiq and I have argued that when two pharmaceutical companies are involved in a patent litigation lawsuit, they should be prohibited from engaging in any linked, unrelated business transactions.[5] Because these side deals are most likely disguised payments to delay entry of a competing product, prohibiting any simultaneous business transaction between the two litigating companies would limit their ability to have the branded firm make unusually large payments to the generic company for unrelated agreements.

At this writing, no such stipulation exists, and the pattern of pharmaceutical companies parasitically creating value by stealing that value from consumers continues. The deals are complex enough that consumers don't pay attention to them; they simply complain about the high cost of drugs. Failing to act on this pattern across cases, the judiciary treats each case as unique and ignores the fact that the payments for the side deals always go from the monopolist to the entrant. Meanwhile, pharmaceutical firms use their profits to lobby Congress and make campaign donations, to discourage legislative changes that would have the power to interrupt their corruption.

By the way, some might be concerned by the simultaneity of me speaking up against corruption, while also getting paid by the FTC as an expert witness. Do I believe my own arguments, or am I simply saying what needs to be said to earn significant fees? This conflict of interest was a concern to me. To resolve it, I have made it a practice to commit to donating 100 percent of the fees from this work to charity, a commitment that is always spelled out in my testimony. This commitment allows me to create value, by both fighting corruption and contributing the proceeds to effective philanthropies.

Rather than simply complaining about the high costs of drugs or saying, "That's just the way it is," we ought to notice corruption like this when it is occurring in our organization, city, state, or country. That means recognizing corruption as more than a bad act. We need to call it out as a behavior that moves us further away from the North Star of creating as much value as possible. How can we do this? We can do this with our vote, our political actions, and our willingness to stand up when corruption exists around us.

CORRUPTION DESTROYS MORAL AUTHORITY

Josh Campbell, a former supervisory special agent for the FBI, described on CNN.com "the power of the nation's brand":

> *Our reputation as a country dedicated to freedom and justice pre-
> cedes all who are honored to identify themselves as American offi-
> cials. While serving diplomatic and operational assignments with
> the FBI in over 20 countries, I saw the power of that brand up close.
> When I spoke, people listened. Not because I was an inordinately
> gifted orator, but rather because I was speaking on behalf of the
> United States government, an imperfect but often emulated con-
> glomeration of agencies known throughout the world as reflecting
> righteousness, fairness, and truth. . . . As one American ambassa-
> dor in South Asia described it to me, we are effective in every corner
> of the globe because of the moral authority generated at home by the
> manner in which we govern ourselves and our commitment to the
> rule of law.[6]*

Moral authority creates trust and allows for greater cooperation, wise trades across countries, and value creation for the United
States and for the world. Thanks in large part to this moral authority, the U.S. government has the power to create lots of value.

By contrast, corruption within government, particularly at the
highest levels, does more than move money from the innocent to
the corrupt; it destroys value and weakens the fabric of society. In
2011, Robert Mueller, then the director of the FBI, reflected on the
high costs society pays for corruption:

> *You might pay more for a gallon of gas. You might pay more for a
> luxury car from overseas. You will pay more for health care, mort-
> gages, clothes, and food. Yet we are concerned with more than just*

the financial impact [of corruption]. These groups may infiltrate our businesses. They may provide logistical support to hostile foreign powers. They may try to manipulate those at the highest levels of government. Indeed, these so-called "iron triangles" of organized criminals, corrupt government officials, and business leaders pose a significant national security threat.[7]

The more corrupt a government is, the more likely perverse incentives are to develop, while the most competent and honest public servants leave government in frustration. Competence gives way to political connections, waste, and incompetence; societal trust is weakened in the process. If government employees are rewarded for supporting corruption, corrupt systems will be institutionalized. Not surprisingly, the countries ranked as the most corrupt in the world are often the poorest and on a downward trajectory.

When government leaders attack our judicial system, and when citizens support these leaders, our nation as a whole sacrifices its moral authority, loses respect, and destroys value. When the White House undermines Special Counsel Robert Mueller's investigation of Russian interference in the 2016 presidential election, the credibility of the U.S. judicial system is damaged. When the president refuses to reduce his own conflicts of interest and instead uses the nation's highest office to enrich his business endeavors, the integrity of the presidency is undermined.

Corruption also puts our national security at risk. Why did the United States invade Afghanistan after 9/11? Most of us would like to believe our leaders were attempting to protect our nation and its allies from further attacks by Al Qaeda. To help create a safer and more prosperous Afghanistan, we helped to install Hamid Karzai as its new leader. Yet in her book *Thieves of State*, Sarah Chayes shows that American tolerance of Afghan corruption, as well as our own corruption, undermined our effectiveness.[8] Chayes documents the enormous corruption of the Afghan government that the United States helped to install, the specific corruption of Hamid Karzai and his family, and the distrust that this corruption created in Afghan society. This corruption provoked resentment, revolts, and even extremist violence, Chayes argues. When the U.S. government accepts and acts in concert with this corruption, the U.S. military presence becomes the focus of citizens' hostility. When we tolerate corrupt behavior from our allies, we lose our moral authority.

From the comfort of the United States, we often wonder how people in other countries could choose groups that we view as clearly corrupt to lead them. But as Chayes highlights, they are often selecting one corrupt entity to replace the corrupt entity that the U.S. government supports. Similarly, in his book *Pay Any Price: Greed, Power, and Endless War*, journalist James Risen details how corrupt payoff schemes by military subcontractors like KBR (formerly a subsidiary of Halliburton) to government officials and their relatives further reduce our government's moral authority and the credibility of our claims that we are there to do good.[9] Contractors may not officially be a part of the U.S. government, but citizens in the countries in which they operate perceive them as such, and they can destroy our moral authority through their actions.

Our government further sacrificed moral authority following the murder of journalist Jamal Khashoggi. Virtually all analysts believe that in 2018, Saudi crown prince Mohammed bin Salman ordered the assassination of journalist Jamal Khashoggi, which occurred when Khashoggi visited the Saudi embassy in Istanbul, Turkey. Khashoggi had been deeply critical of the Saudi regime, and the United States has viewed Saudi Arabia as a critical ally in a very difficult part of the world.

Soon after the murder, Turkish authorities released intelligence showing that the prince was behind the murder. Intelligence operations across the globe, including the CIA, were convinced that the prince had authorized the murder. Yet even after all of this evidence was in, President Trump declared strong support for Saudi Arabia. Trump obfuscated by noting that U.S. intelligence would continue to assess the story and by saying that we "may never know all the facts surrounding the murder."[10] Addressing the question of whether the crown prince knew about or ordered the killing, Trump said, "Maybe he did or maybe he didn't!"[11] Trump's position did not change even after the *New York Times* reported that U.S. intelligence had a recording of Prince Mohammed telling an aide in September 2017 that he would go after Mr. Khashoggi "with a bullet" if he didn't return to the kingdom and end his criticism of the Saudi government.[12]

Trump further indicated that Saudi oil production, purchases of weapons from the United States, and support for U.S. policies in the Middle East were more important to him than holding Saudi Arabia accountable for the murder of a journalist. "I'm not going to destroy our economy by being foolish with Saudi Arabia," he said.[13] Obviously, there was a short-term strategic benefit to not confronting our ally about its leader's brutality and illegality, but Trump failed to understand or care about the long-term ramifications of continuing to chip away at American moral authority.

Moral authority belongs not only to government leaders, but to all of us. Patients are more likely to trust and follow the instructions of doctors who act with integrity. Negotiators who have moral authority more easily exchange information, find value-creating trades, and develop better relationships as compared to those who don't. The moral authority of nonprofit leaders increases trust in the organization and facilitates fundraising and creative, effective, and efficient solutions to societal problems. And the moral authority of corporate leaders allows them to contribute the best that business has to offer society. In all of these realms, however, sacrificing moral authority inflicts damage far beyond the initial unethical behavior, reducing value for society as a result of the loss of trust in the person or the broader institution.

BUYING THE LAWS YOU WANT

Americans are often (rightfully) critical of other nations. We often criticize emerging economies where illegal behavior interferes with the operation of honest markets. We criticize nations where bribery of public officials is common. Yet we are less critical when our own leaders participate in corrupt actions that distort our laws in ways that favor special-interest groups and the leaders themselves over the public as a whole. Essentially, we have created a political system that allows corruption by distorting the law rather than breaking it.

The abuses that occur in the payday loan industry provide a glaring example of the way in which our political system can promote corruption. By offering short-term loans as advances on wages, payday loan companies provide the working poor and others suffering financial hardship with a means of obtaining emergency cash. In the best of circumstances, the consumer is able to repay the loan on her next payday. Yet payday loans, which have been available for about twenty-five years, carry interest rates ranging from 200 to 500 percent per year, and the average payday borrower takes out eight loans a year. On an average payday loan of $375, borrowers pay an average $520 in interest. While payday lenders and the lobbyists they hire to represent them in Washington claim they are meeting a need in low-income areas not served by traditional lending institutions, consumer advocates and independent analyses argue that these loans do far more harm than good. Most payday borrowers are unable to repay their debts in time and are left to choose between defaulting on their loans or borrowing more money and escalating their financial woes.

During the Obama administration, many states moved to regulate and in some cases ban payday lending, and the industry downsized. In addition, abuses in the payday loan industry partly inspired the Wall Street Reform and Consumer Protection Act, which President Obama signed into law in 2009. The act, which created the Consumer Financial Protection Bureau (CFPB), was intended to protect and educate consumers about payday lending, banking, securities firms, debt collectors, and other financial businesses. In 2013, the CFPB accused payday lenders of "trapping borrowers in a cycle of debt."[14]

While the CFPB was politically volatile, having been largely created by a very liberal senator, Elizabeth Warren of Massachusetts, few politicians actively or publicly supported payday lenders. Yet since the election of Trump, payday lenders have corruptly purchased political changes that have improved their profitability while causing massive additional harm to borrowers. To head the CFPB, Trump installed Mick Mulvaney, a former congressman who received more than $60,000 in campaign contributions from payday lenders. Mulvaney was an outspoken supporter of the payday loan industry, yet he was chosen to oversee it.

What came next is, sadly, not surprising, given Mulvaney's glaring conflict of interest: he scrapped tough new regulations aimed at protecting borrowers from payday loans. The CFPB shouldn't need to regulate the industry (despite having been created in part to do so), he argued, because "[t]he best way to address the problem that you perceive is to pass legislation and not rely on me to do it for you." Mulvaney, of course, knew full well that the Republican Congress in power at the time would never pass such legislation. Since his statements and regulatory changes to the industry, stocks for publicly traded payday lenders have shot up.

Around this time, the Community Financial Services Association of America, the trade group for payday lenders, booked its annual conference at Trump National Doral, a Miami golf resort that the Trump Organization bought out of bankruptcy in 2012 and renovated for $150 million with $125 million in loans from Deutsche Bank. Dennis Shaul, the leader of the trade group, claimed that golf and good weather motivated the decision to hold the conference at a Trump property, not politics—but, of course, there are plenty of nice golf resorts to choose from in Florida.

Generally, when you see economic systems that don't seem to be maximizing value for society, you will find the corrupting influence of special-interest-group politics nearby. These special-interest groups and the politicians beholden to them are parasitically siphoning off value that should be going to consumers and citizens. Long before Trump became president, special-interest groups had been moving in the opposite direction from the utilitarian North Star.

Many industries lobby for their own interests in completely legal ways, including industries that don't face media scrutiny. Consider the field of independent auditing (I know most readers find auditing to be a boring topic, but hang on). All developed economies believe that external parties (investors, strategic partners, etc.) need to be able to rely on a company's financial reporting when making decisions and view independent auditing as a structure that enables them to do so. As then chief justice Warren Burger wrote in *United States v. Arthur Young & Co.* in 1984:

> *By certifying the public reports that collectively depict a corporation's financial status, the independent auditor assumes a public responsibility transcending any employment relationship with the*

client. The independent public accountant performing this special function owes ultimate allegiance to the corporation's creditors and stockholders, as well as to the investing public. This "public watch-dog" function demands that the accountant maintain total inde-pendence from the client at all times and requires complete fidelity to the public trust.[15]

There are currently four firms large enough to audit the very largest corporations in society, after a fifth, Arthur Andersen, was forced to go out of business following its failure to notice Enron's malpractices. The only reason for audit firms to exist is to provide independent audits, yet the auditing industry in the United States was set up in a manner that effectively eliminates independence in auditing. Auditing firms have financial incentives to avoid being fired by their clients. If an audit firm questions the client's finan-cials, the client has an incentive to find a new auditor, and the auditor loses a client. Audit firms also make significant additional profit from selling non-audit services (that is, consulting services) to their auditing clients, and individual auditors very often end up taking jobs with client firms. As a result, identifying problems with the client's books can eliminate a career opportunity for the auditor. After a thorough investigation of these conflicts of inter-est, my colleagues and I long ago concluded that auditing firms do not live up to their promise of being independent.[16]

Creating the type of auditor independence needed to protect our financial markets would require that auditing firms only audit and not provide other services; that companies would regularly switch auditors; and that individual auditors would be barred from accepting positions with client firms for a set number of years.[17] But we haven't been able to get there, despite the value that such a proposal would create for society. The Sarbanes-Oxley Act of 2002 was intended to move in the direction of reform but was a weak attempt, watered down by political compromises. The primary reason we're stuck with a corrupt system is the willingness of the large auditing firms to spend millions of dollars lobbying against reforms that would be good for investors, good for audited companies, and good for our financial system's moral integrity. The only parties that have a long-term stake in keeping the current system in its current corrupt form are the four firms that currently provide services to the vast majority of large corporations.

These four firms work hard to send a false message about their ability to provide independent audits. In July 2000, just a little more than a year before the collapse of Enron, whose accounting irregularities Arthur Andersen failed to report, Andersen managing partner Joseph Berardino provided the following written testimony to an SEC hearing aimed at exploring measures to improve auditor independence:

> The future of the [accounting] profession is bright and will remain bright—as long as the Commission does not force us into an outdated role trapped in the old economy. Unfortunately, the proposed rule [on auditor independence] threatens to do exactly that. A broad scope of practice is critical to enable us to keep up with the new business environment, attract, motivate and keep top talent, and thereby provide high quality audits in the future.

The testimony and lobbying of most of the Big Five audit firms kept the SEC from instituting reform, and it continues to do so to this day—even after Arthur Andersen's demise due to its failure to provide exactly what Berardino promised.

What is fascinating and relatively unique about this story is that the auditing industry exists explicitly to help reduce corporate corruption, yet its own corrupt behavior prevents us from creating an auditing industry that could actually deliver on this promise. Ideally, government officials would make decisions that were in the best interest of the overall society, and it is hard to imagine that society would benefit from an auditing institution that fails in its mission to be independent. But in the United States, special-interest groups (including the auditing industry) lobby to write our laws and buy our politicians at levels that are unheard-of in the rest of the world.

This corruption has only increased since the Supreme Court's 2010 *Citizens United v. Federal Election Commission* decision, which overturned restrictions on independent expenditures from corporations and labor unions for political communications and election spending. The infamous decision spawned the creation of so-called super PACs, which can accept unlimited contributions from corporations, unions, and other groups. Since then, campaign funding has increasingly shifted toward super PACs and "dark money" political nonprofits, unleashing unprecedented amounts of money to contort the laws in favor of special interests. Citizens and corporations in the United States may be more law-abiding than those in many other countries, yet no country has corrupted the lawmaking process at the level of the United States.[18] But across nations, corruption has created rampant and unethical value destruction, regardless of whether laws are actually being broken.

CORRUPTION THROUGH MISINFORMATION

The tobacco and energy (most specifically coal and oil) industries may destroy more value than all other industries combined. Tobacco killed about 100 million people in the twentieth century and will kill many times that number in the twenty-first century. Climate change, exacerbated by coal and oil production, may ultimately kill more people than tobacco. Interestingly, the energy industry relies on misinformation methods very similar to those employed by the tobacco industry decades earlier. In our book, *Blind Spots: Why We Fail to Do What's Right and What to Do about It*, Ann Tenbrunsel and I highlight the strategies that industries use to corrupt our understanding of science and destroy value in the process.[19]

Obfuscation

Corporations that want to delay societally beneficial reforms obfuscate, communicating in a deliberately confusing or ambiguous manner with the intention of misleading the listener. To avoid or slow down antismoking measures, the tobacco industry fomented confusion about the health effects of smoking for decades after finding out about the harm its products caused. While many oil companies pollute, Exxon Mobil was predominant in misleading the public by obfuscating the existence of climate change and the role of humans in creating the problem by burning fossil fuels. Big Tobacco and Exxon Mobil are well aware that obfuscation creates uncertainty—and that the public is less willing to invest in solving a problem whose existence or severity is uncertain than one that most certainly poses a significant threat.

Encouraging Reasonable Doubt

For forty years, from the 1950s to the 1990s, Big Tobacco maintained an explicit strategy of sowing doubt in the minds of smokers about the adverse health effects of cigarettes, long after there was scientific clarity about the causal role of cigarettes in lung cancer. Similarly, long after a clear consensus existed among scientists who were not being paid for their views, Exxon Mobil spent enormous amounts of time and money communicating to the public that some experts doubted the existence of climate change and, if it did exist, the role that humans played in it. Such carefully planted seeds of doubt make it difficult for politicians to act and for citizens to mobilize in support of reform.

Expressing Shifting Views of the Facts

To make a strong case to the public and politicians, corrupting forces insist upon their own distorted view of the "facts." When their positions become untenable, they simply change their position and deny their past connection to claims that they now acknowledge, in the face of overwhelming evidence, to be clearly false. For decades, the tobacco industry held fast to the view that cigarettes caused no harm, and indeed might even achieve some positive health benefits, such as weight control, improved digestion, and relaxation. As the scientific connection between lung cancer and cigarettes mounted, industry executives grudgingly acknowledged that cigarettes might be one of many possible causes of lung cancer but insisted that no specific cancer could be traced to cigarettes and that the causal path was unclear. Exxon-Mobil made a relatively rapid shift in recent years: from insisting that man-made global warming did not exist, to claiming global warming is not caused by human actions, to arguing that it would not be worth the enormous costs to fix the problem. Maintaining the most reactionary view that is defensible and shifting their positions only out of necessity allows the enemies of wise policies to delay change and profit during the delay.

Maintaining the Status Quo

Psychologists have long known that, when contemplating a potential change, we tend to be more concerned about the risk of change than about the risk of failing to change. Imagine, for instance, that you receive an offer for a job that is much better than your current job on some dimensions (pay, responsibility, etc.) and marginally worse on others (location, health insurance, etc.). A rational analysis would imply that if the evident gains exceed the expected losses, you should accept the new job. However, the psychological tendency to pay more attention to losses than to gains will lead many to turn down the job, preserve the status quo, and forgo a net gain. Because losses loom larger than gains psychologically, the status quo creates inertia that is a barrier to wise action. The desire to maintain the status quo has a powerful impact on our decisions and interacts with the other obstructionist techniques I've described to keep society from acting.

What can we do to create value as citizens? We need to support politicians who accept science as a basis for policy and who are wise and brave enough to advocate to create value for society. We also need to support dramatic campaign finance reform. We should reward politicians who are ready to prevent corporations and industries from standing in the way of wise decisions for those they were elected to serve. We should elect leaders who will seek to punish organizations and industries that commit crimes that destroy value with the full power of the law.

EVERYDAY CORRUPTION

Most of the examples I've described in this chapter have involved truly egregious corruption. Notably, much of this behavior doesn't break any laws; in many cases, the corruption occurs when corporations lobby for laws that benefit the few at the expense of broader society. I personally find each of the major stories that I have written about disturbing and disappointing. I am frustrated that our society allows these events to unfold as they do. The downside of focusing on these visible episodes, however, is that it is easy to distance ourselves from these corrupt acts and to assume that we are innocent ourselves. And, in many cases that confront us in ordinary life, corruption is not as clear or corrosive, yet still important.

In her book *Cheating: Ethics in Everyday Life*, Stanford law professor Deborah Rhode describes just how widespread cheating is in society, a phenomenon she illustrates with stories of cheating from the realms of sports, business, paying taxes, plagiarism, copyright infringement, insurance claims, and marriage.[20] As you are thinking about any type of cheating you might have done in life, such as not reporting a small amount of income on your taxes or downloading a pirated video, note that it is common to rationalize these acts on the grounds that "everybody does it." But note that these acts are more common and socially acceptable in some societies than in others. When we engage in them, we diffuse these corrupt acts by normalizing them.

To show how this normalization can happen, Rhode cites the repeated acts of corruption that have been documented in Trump's businesses, including his development business and his $25 million settlement of a fraud case brought against Trump University. Only one-third of Americans believe that Trump is honest, yet he received 46.1 percent of the vote (Hillary Clinton received 48.2 percent). Collectively, we know he is corrupt, yet we seem to not care. This lack of concern about the corruption of our leaders is a problem, as it signals to the next generation of leaders that honesty is optional.

Attempting the difficult task of estimating the costs that cheating inflicts on society, Rhode comes up with a number of around $1 trillion per year in the United States alone. That figure includes $450 billion from the underpayment of taxes, $250 billion from illegal downloads, another couple hundred billion from insurance fraud, and anywhere from $50 billion to $200 billion from employee theft. These estimates are probably on the low side, given that people work hard to conceal their cheating. In any case, the real numbers are clearly huge. Not only do deserving parties fail to receive the funds they deserve, but the cheater becomes a lesser person as a result of his or her corruption. Perhaps most important, institutions that run the government, encourage innovation, enable insurance coverage, and so on are compromised.

FIXING CORRUPTION

Insurance is an unusually simple business. The basic idea is that you pay premiums regularly so that if something bad happens, you can submit a claim and receive a payment from the insurance company for the costs you incur. That's it: pay money in the form of premiums, and receive money when you make a claim. The industry has no physical products to make or complex services to provide. Yet, walk around London, New York, or Zurich, and you will notice that insurance companies occupy very big buildings, sometimes multiple very big buildings. So, what are all the employees inside doing? Based on my experience, many are spending a great amount of time not paying claims.

That's right—I said not paying claims. Large insurers often dedicate thousands of employees to assessing and negotiating with claimants, with a focus on paying less money than the claimant requested (or demanded). Why not pay the claim? The insurance adjusters are quick to explain that it is because people lie—and sometimes lie a great deal. They add items to their list of what was stolen and exaggerate the value of items. They overstate their injuries. Fraud is a major problem confronting the insurance industry, and insurance firms spend many millions of dollars each year on fraud detection. Meanwhile, if you ask claimants why they are asking for more than the objective value of the claim, they are likely to reply that the insurance company views the claim as a starting point for negotiation, and if you are honest, you will end up with less than the objective value of the claim. Thus, both sides end up acting in a corrupt manner to counter the expected corruption of the other side. One large insurance company that I know well devotes about three thousand claims adjusters and spends about $3 billion (yes, billion) on external legal fees to pay about $30 billion in claims. All of this hassle, cost, and value destruction is caused by mutually destructive corruption. Is this "just the way it is," or can something be done to create value?

As I was getting to know the insurance industry while consulting with one of the world's largest insurers, I was also the fifth author on a paper that starts with the words "Signing at the Beginning . . ."[21] Think about the tax form you fill out annually, or any expense reimbursement forms you've filled out in the past. You'll remember that after filling out such forms, you're typically asked to sign your name to attest that you completed the form honestly. In this initial paper on signing first, my coauthors and I found that if people promise to tell the truth *before* filling out a form—that is, at the top of the form rather than the bottom, or on the first screen of an online form rather than the last—they fill out the form far more honestly than if they sign it after.

The paper was published in the *Proceedings of the National Academy of Sciences (PNAS)*, not exactly the best place to get the attention of start-up entrepreneurs or insurance executives.[22] Making matters worse, we recently failed to replicate this result, reducing my confidence in the conclusion of the paper.[23] However, I did receive an email from a start-up insurance executive by the name of Stuart Baserman, who had read the original *PNAS* article. Stu had an interest in getting people to tell the truth online. Stu is low-key, but based on our nearly identical and rather uncommon last names and the topic of my paper, his spouse, Sue, pushed him to send me an email, which led to a friendship and a work relationship.

Stu is the cofounder of a company called Slice.[24] If you go to their website, you will see that they are in the business of selling short-term insurance to people who rent out their homes on Airbnb or Homeaway. The insurance covers the residential property when it's being used for commercial purposes. Most relevant, Slice sells the vast majority of its policies online and handles claims online. In the process, Slice has become a leader in helping large companies think through how to sell policies and pay claims online with far greater efficiency than the traditional model. Slice can handle claims at a far lower cost than traditional insurance firms. But, it may have occurred to you that claimants might be more likely to lie in an online world?

That's where I came in. After Stu contacted me, thinking that I might know something about how to get people to tell the truth, Slice hired me as a consultant to help devise the claims process in a manner that would reduce fraud. Imagine a world where claimants told their insurance company the truth, and the company honestly paid the claim. Most of the $3 billion that at least one company has been spending on legal fees wouldn't be needed. Thousands of claims adjusters could be replaced by tens of claims adjusters. Claims could be paid far faster, and claimants (often also called customers) could be far happier with their insurance provider.

How to create this utopian world of insurance? To start with, the goal isn't complete honesty—any more than our goal in this book is to be perfect—but rather far less corruption than occurs currently. In addition, like so many other aspects of today's economy, insurance will need to move onto the cell phones that govern so much of the rest of our lives. What would be key ingredients to the online claims service? Slice is still working on it, but here are some hints.

First, very good artificial intelligence (based on past claims and other aspects of claimants' lives that can be found online) would be used to identify the small portion of claims that are actually completely fraudulent. Next, when a customer incurs an insured loss, she would simply open up the app on her phone and fill out a claim form. She would commit to telling the truth before filling out the rest of the form, in order to induce an honesty mindset. In addition, the claimant would be asked to create a very short video using her phone's camera describing her claim as simply as possible. Why? Because people are far less likely to lie in a video than when writing or typing. Claimants would then be asked specific, verifiable questions about the loss, such as "What did you pay for the lost object?" or "What does it cost to replace it on Amazon.com?" rather than "What was it worth?" That's obviously because more general questions allow people to provide more ambiguous answers, which are more likely to be deceptive. Next, claimants would be asked who else knows about the loss (such as a guest who was in the house when the loss occurred). People are less likely to be deceptive when their corruption could be communicated to others. Assuming the artificial intelligence assesses the claim to be trustworthy, the typical claim would then be paid within moments, thanks to an automated payment system. By paying claims so honestly and efficiently, the insurance company will gain a reputation for being trustworthy, and, thanks to the psychology of reciprocation, customers will be more honest in return. The goal is to create a fundamentally more competitive insurance product that is better for honest customers and better for the insurer as well—true value creation.

I feel fortunate to have had the opportunity to spend my time trying to reduce corruption on a potentially broad scale. I like the idea of helping to create a more honest insurance system. But there is much that *all* of us can do to create value by reducing corruption. One obvious step is to avoid the temptation to be corrupt, even when everyone else is doing it. But, given that you are probably pretty honest, or you wouldn't have read this far in this book, you probably have bigger opportunities to notice and act when others are being corrupt. Elsewhere, I have written in detail about Bernard Madoff's Ponzi scheme, which involved him stealing tens of billions of dollars from unsuspecting investors.[25] For me, the most interesting part of the story is not that a really bad guy did bad things, but that hundreds of bright, well-educated people had the data in front of them showing that Madoff's returns were impossible, but didn't notice and act on this information. So, in the future, when you see something that seems off or too good to be true, remember your obligation to speak up and make the world a better place.

CHAPTER 5

ACTIVATING YOUR MORAL OBLIGATION TO NOTICE

The last three chapters have focused on the potential you have to create more value by more actively engaging your intelligence, finding trade-offs to create value, and more effectively inducing honesty. In order to use these skills, you will often need to notice that an opportunity to create value exists. This chapter highlights the challenge of noticing opportunities to create value. Vigilance and skill are needed to notice the need for action.

To get us started, I'm going to challenge you with an investment decision that I often present to MBA students, executives, investment bankers, and a host of other elite groups:[1]

Imagine that you are an investment advisor for a client who has a long-term investment perspective and a moderate tolerance for risk. You are considering one of four investment funds for this client: the Tobacco Trade Investments Fund, the Alpha Investments Fund, the Fortitude Investments Fund, or the Power Trade

Investments Fund. The figure below provides the returns for each of the funds over the last nine years, as well as the average returns for the S&P 500.

Which fund do you recommend?

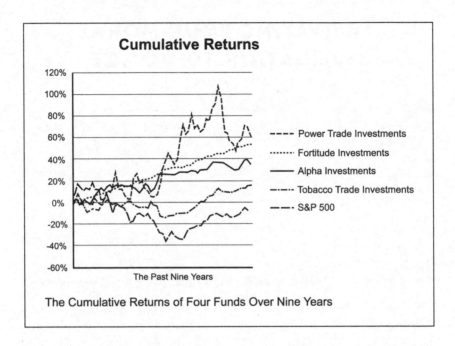

The Cumulative Returns of Four Funds Over Nine Years

Most people have little interest in the lowest-performing fund of the four, which also invests in an undesirable industry. Of the remaining three, the vast majority, including those with investment expertise, opt for Fortitude. However, when the same people are asked if they see a problem with any of the funds, many participants are quick to note that Fortitude's returns are impossible. Basic finance education tells people that no fund can outperform the market over a nine-year period without volatility. Asking participants if a problem exists brings this fact to light quickly, even though when the same people were focused on picking an investment, they concentrated on returns and low volatility.

Asking participants which fund to recommend leads to what my colleague Ann Tenbrunsel calls ethical fading, or the tendency of the ethical elements of a decision to fade from our attention when our attention is diverted elsewhere.[2] By the way, if you picked Fortitude, your choice went bankrupt, as you invested in a feeder fund that invested all of its funds in Bernie Madoff's Ponzi scheme. And you made this choice despite the hint I gave you at the close of the prior chapter when I mentioned the Madoff scandal.

It's worth noting that most of the investments that ended up with Madoff came through feeder funds: these feeder funds sold investments to their retail customers, then reinvested their funds with Madoff. Bernie Madoff didn't invest the money that investors were entrusting him with—he simply stole the money and used some of it for administration and to repay the minority of investors who took their money out before the fund collapsed. Madoff's investors lost as much as $65 billion in his Ponzi scheme.

Many readers of this book may not have the financial background required to know that Madoff's returns on investment were impossible. But many individuals who had ample expertise and intelligence to know that dramatically outperforming the market over nine years with very little volatility was impossible nonetheless recommended Madoff's fund. These professionals had the knowledge that they needed to make a sound decision; they just didn't connect that knowledge to the data that was readily available and often right in front of them. Even after Madoff's collapse, I doubt that these investment professionals recognized that their failure to notice the impossibility of his returns was an ethical issue. Yet this failure to notice allowed massive harm to occur. The failure to notice destroys value.

Recognizing threats that could destroy value for you and for the rest of the world is an important skill. I believe that when an individual has the knowledge and the intelligence needed to notice unethical conduct and the power to act on it, they have a moral obligation to do so. Madoff could not have perpetuated his fraud without the contributions of financial experts who should have known better. As we'll see, the failure to notice likely threats is common, and value destruction often follows. In addition, the failure to notice affects all of us, including some very impressive people. Fortunately, there are actions we can all take to do a better job of noticing.

TAKING POSITIONS OF RESPONSIBILITY
MAKES YOU ACCOUNTABLE TO NOTICE

The following famous men have very impressive credentials and are known for their intelligence:

Henry Kissinger served as U.S. secretary of state and national security advisor under the presidential administrations of Richard Nixon and Gerald Ford. While controversial, he was widely viewed as brilliant.

George Shultz is one of just two individuals to hold four different U.S. cabinet positions, serving under three different Republican presidents. He played a major role in shaping the foreign policy of the Ronald Reagan administration.

General James "Mad Dog" Mattis served in the U.S. Marine Corps and as the twenty-sixth secretary of defense from January 2017 through December 2018. Known as an intellectual, he resigned over policy differences with President Donald Trump.

William James Perry is an American mathematician, engineer, and businessman who was the U.S. secretary of defense under President Bill Clinton. Perry was a professor at Stanford University, a senior fellow at Stanford's Hoover Institution, a member of the National Academy of Engineering, and a fellow of the American Academy of Arts and Sciences.

Sam Nunn served for twenty-four years as a U.S. Democratic senator from Georgia (1973 until 1997). His political experience and credentials on national defense reportedly earned him consideration as a potential running mate for presidential candidates John Kerry (2004) and Barack Obama (2008).

What else do these men have in common, aside from their impressive political credentials and keen intellect? They all served on the board of Theranos, one of the most well-known medical companies of the twenty-first century, though they all lacked knowledge about medical technology. In addition, they were all negligent in failing to notice fraud that was right in front of them, fraud that cost Theranos investors hundreds of millions of dollars, generated false diagnoses for tens of thousands of patients, and misled and misdirected the health-care world in a shocking manner.

In 2004, Elizabeth Holmes dropped out of Stanford at age nineteen to found Theranos, a company that sought to revolutionize the blood-testing process. Holmes claimed to offer a breakthrough technology that was more efficient and less invasive than current blood draws via syringe. According to Holmes, the revolutionary new technology had the potential to conduct up to two hundred different blood tests using less than a hundredth of the amount of blood that would ordinarily be needed, obtained from just the prick of a finger. Holmes falsely and repeatedly claimed that Theranos could perform these blood tests using a small, portable, automated lab (called the Edison) that would reduce human error and offer faster results, all at a lower cost.

Theranos raised more than $700 million in start-up funds from investors, and the company's market value peaked at over $9 billion in 2013–14. Holmes was on *Time* magazine's list of the one hundred most influential people in 2015; the same year, *Glamour* magazine named her its "Woman of the Year." But in October 2015, tipped off by sources within Theranos, *Wall Street Journal* reporter John Carreyrou wrote an article questioning the validity of the company's technology. A series of legal and commercial challenges followed from medical authorities, investors, the U.S. Securities and Exchange Commission (SEC), the U.S. Centers for Medicare and Medicaid Services (which provides oversight of medical labs), state attorneys general, former business partners, patients, and others. Collectively, they unearthed the massive fraud that has been well documented in Carreyrou's book *Bad Blood* and in films and podcasts.[3] By June 2016, Holmes's personal net worth had dropped from $4.5 billion to virtually nothing.

On March 14, 2018, the SEC charged Theranos, Holmes, and the company's former president (and Holmes's romantic partner at the time) Ramesh "Sunny" Balwani with "massive fraud." The SEC complaint claimed that Holmes had falsely stated that the company had annual revenues of $100 million, a thousand times more than the actual figure of $100,000. This was just one of many lies that Holmes and Balwani told its board, its investors, and the media. Theranos and Holmes agreed to resolve these civil charges, with Holmes paying a fine of $500,000, returning the remaining 18.9 million shares that she held, relinquishing her control of the company, and being barred from being an officer or director of any public company for ten years. Balwani did not settle.

On June 15, 2018, the U.S. attorney for the Northern District of California announced the indictments of Holmes and Balwani on wire fraud and conspiracy charges.[4] After all efforts to find a buyer for Theranos went nowhere, what remained of the company dissolved on September 4, 2018. The trial is expected to begin in August 2020.[5]

Criminals will always be among us; social scientists have provided little new insight on how to stop their behavior. Evidence suggests that Holmes started with the typical exaggerations that are common in Silicon Valley, then slowly escalated her commitment to her claims as threats and opportunities emerged. This slippery slope toward massive corruption was also apparent in Madoff's behavior. But these criminals are not our focus. Rather, our focus is on the many people, including Theranos board members, investors, business partners, and regulators, who didn't notice the plentiful signs of fraud at Theranos until Carreyrou did.

The board of directors of Theranos was an impressive group of people, but it wasn't an appropriate board for a company of its valuation. The board members achieved their fame in areas far removed from medical technology, and they obtained that fame during a very different era. They lacked auditing and legal expertise. There was also a shocking lack of scientific and medical knowledge across the entire board. Theranos is the story of how a very smart, deceptive leader fooled many older, powerful men who had little knowledge that was actually relevant to Theranos's business. Holmes had little expertise of her own in medicine or business; the board added even less. Board members were never asked to use their connections for scientific or medical advice, only to identify the next group of investors who could be suckered by Holmes's act. The composition of the board should have been a warning that something was amiss, but it wasn't the only warning.

Secrecy was extreme at Theranos. This was, in part, normal for a high-tech firm with an exciting new technology; it was understandable that employees were asked to sign nondisclosure agreements. But other elements of this secrecy were not normal. Most biotech firms take pride in being connected to the scientific community; Theranos avoided such contact like the plague. The company avoided soliciting peer reviews, outside expertise, or observations from outside parties. In one now-infamous quote, Holmes described how Theranos's technology worked: "A chemistry is performed so that a chemical reaction occurs and generates a signal from the chemical interaction with the sample, which is translated into a result, which is then reviewed by certified laboratory personnel." Despite the consistent presentation of such vacuous statements, the company's board and others continued to keep their heads in the sand.

Professor Phyllis Gardner, an advisor to Holmes at Stanford's School of Medicine, moved beyond skepticism to explicitly tell Holmes and others that what Theranos was trying to do wasn't physically possible. Despite this scientific assessment, Holmes entered into agreements with multiple major pharmaceutical firms that were contingent on the results of tests conducted to validate the Theranos technology. After conducting the first failed test of the technology in 2006, the Switzerland-based pharmaceutical firm Novartis cut off contact with Theranos. Pfizer walked away from Theranos the following year when a test it conducted showed inconsistent and erratic results. The failures mounted, yet despite the lack of any external confirmation of the scientific validity of Theranos's method, board members, investors, and others failed to notice.

Theranos staff who asked critical questions about the product were threatened, ostracized, and demoted. When the company's CFO learned about the Novartis failure in 2006 and suggested that Theranos might be misrepresenting its data, he was criticized for not being a team player and fired. Another internal critic, Ian Gibbons, committed suicide as a result of the abuse he suffered within Theranos. Different departments within Theranos were prohibited from coordinating with each other, even when such coordination was simply logical. Investors were told they would not be provided with regular updates about developments within

Theranos. Lacking scientific and medical knowledge, they weren't bothered by the lack of detail; rather, they were comforted by the other famous people who were persuaded by Holmes's pitch.

The members of the board of directors and others should have noticed Theranos's fraud well in advance of Carreyrou's *Wall Street Journal* article. But this noticing story isn't as simple as the story of Madoff's returns, which were simply impossible. Rather, multiple alarms should have been sounded. Theranos had an inappropriate board that lacked competence for the task at hand; its secrecy didn't make sense; the science behind the technology failed at multiple steps along the way; and leaders imposed authoritarian control on employees and information. Far too often, when most of us see hints that we cannot fully explain, we fail to ask questions that highlight our ignorance and instead focus on problems where we have greater expertise. In contrast, when we have responsibility to provide oversight, these hints should serve as a prompt for us to demand clearer accountability.

NOT NOTICING IS NOT A GOOD EXCUSE

A German, Carl Benz, invented the automobile. Thus, it was frustrating to many Germans that it was an American, Henry Ford, who made car ownership affordable. In 1938, one in fifty Germans owned a car, while in the United States, the ratio was one in five.[6] In 1937, the German government, led by Adolf Hitler and the National Socialist (Nazi) Party, created a new state-owned automobile company called Volkswagenwerk, or "The People's Car Company." Seeking to develop an affordable yet still speedy vehicle, Hitler hired Austrian automotive engineer Ferdinand Porsche to design the car. The car was introduced at the Berlin Motor Show in 1939, but after World War II began, Volkswagen (VW) halted production. During the war, the Volkswagen facility was repurposed for producing weapons and became the Nazis' largest user of slave labor, including prisoners at the Auschwitz concentration camp. Many workers were killed in the course of their work.

After the war ended and the factory was in ruins, the Allies (led by the British, who were in charge of that part of Germany) made VW the focus of their attempts to resuscitate the German auto industry. VW sales in the United States were initially slower than in other parts of the world due to the car's Nazi connections, as well as its small size and unusual rounded shape. Then, in 1959, an American advertising agency launched a landmark campaign, dubbing the car the "Beetle" and spinning its diminutive size as a distinct advantage to consumers. Over the next several years, VW became the top-selling auto import in the United States and was particularly popular with the countercultural movement of the 1960s. I owned a VW car in the mid-1970s, a Karmann Ghia, which I bought used for seven hundred dollars. It looked like a squashed beetle, but was more or less the shape of a sports car. I liked the car, although some of my friends and family questioned the ethics of owning a car with Nazi roots. For me, that history was part of the distant past.

More recent VW history was dominated by the authoritarian influence of CEO Ferdinand Piëch, Ferdinand Porsche's grandson. He reigned over VW's supervisory board and, upon becoming CEO of VW in 1993, set the goal of making VW the world's largest automaker. Piëch bragged that he obtained superior performance by "terrifying his engineers." During Piëch's reign, many unethical and illegal actions occurred at VW. Two were quite famous. One involved the hiring of the famous procurement expert Jose Ignacio Lopez de Arriortua from General Motors in 1993. While poaching senior executives from other firms is common and legal, General Motors and a number of law enforcement agencies accused Piëch and VW of industrial espionage. Specifically, they were accused of engaging with Lopez and direct reports who had come with him from GM in a coordinated effort to copy and steal GM documents. The dispute was settled out of court, with VW paying General Motors $100 million and agreeing to buy $1 billion in GM parts.

The second visible scandal, in 2005, involved VW management spending more than $5 million on prostitution for themselves and labor leaders with the goal of keeping the labor leaders happy with existing management plans.[7] Piëch was never proved to be at the center of these scandals, but he didn't raise them as ethical issues to be worried about, either. Under Piëch, employees broadly understood that they were expected to get their work done regardless of the methods needed to achieve specified goals.[8]

Piëch gave up his CEO role in 2002, maintained his position as the head of VW's supervisory board, and pushed through his choice to succeed him as CEO, Bernd Pischetsrieder. As it turned out, Pischetsrieder had more of a moral compass than Piëch, was less dictatorial, cared more about getting worker input, and was interested in using VW's scandal-ridden history to redirect the firm. The fact that this could mean investigating past scandals led workers, the supervisory board, and Piëch to lose enthusiasm for his leadership. Despite achieving excellent financial results, Pischetsrieder was not reappointed at the end of his first five-year term.

In 2007, the CEO position went to Martin Winterkorn, who had been a protégé of Piëch's for thirty years. Maintaining the goal of becoming the world's largest automaker, Winterkorn reestablished Piëch's authoritarian style and his focus on getting results at any cost—including an ethical cost. Winterkorn didn't like bad news, and during his reign, employees who later left the company described a workplace in which subordinates were afraid to admit failure or contradict their superiors. Winterkorn saw the U.S. market as having the greatest potential for growth, which led to a focus on creating a "clean" diesel engine whose emissions could pass America's increasingly stringent pollution regulations. VW engineers and engineers at Audi, a VW subsidiary, were put under enormous pressure to develop a solution—one that was either not in their skill set or simply not physically possible. When people are given difficult goals and cannot achieve them legally, they become more likely to engage in illegal activities to do so.[9] VW produced and advertised a set of "clean diesel" cars that became popular among environmentally conscious consumers in the United States and around the world.

I became aware of VW's recent unethical behavior in 2015. In 2014, the California Air Resources Board (CARB) commissioned a study on emissions discrepancies between lab and on-the-road emissions. One of the teams hired by CARB, a group of five scientists at West Virginia University, was the first to detect an inconsistency between how VW's software operated during testing versus when cars were actually being driven. These inconsistencies led regulators from numerous countries to begin investigations. In September 2015, the U.S. Environmental Protection Agency (EPA) issued a notice of violation of the Clean Air Act to VW. The EPA accused VW of intentionally programming its diesel engines to activate their emissions controls only during laboratory emissions testing and not when the vehicle was in normal use. In the test mode, the cars register as being in compliance with all U.S. federal emissions regulations. When not in test mode, during normal driving, the cars switch to a different mode in which the fuel pressure, injection timing, and exhaust-gas recirculation are dramatically different. This regular mode delivers higher mileage and power, but also permits much more nitrogen oxide emissions (NOx), up to forty times higher than the federal limit. NOx is a smog-forming pollutant strongly linked to lung cancer, asthma, and other maladies.

To fool regulators, VW engineers intentionally created a device that would pollute our air and result in the deaths of thousands of people.[10] This intentional deception lured millions of people worldwide to buy the VW product specifically to be good environmentalists. Approximately eleven million of the cars were sold worldwide in model years 2009 through 2015, more than 500,000 of them in the United States.

After the deception was revealed, Volkswagen CEO Martin Winterkorn resigned, and a number of other leaders were suspended. On September 29, 2015, Volkswagen announced plans to repair up to 11 million vehicles. VW claimed that all affected cars would be fixed by the end of 2015. Yet, the recall wasn't scheduled to start until January 2016. And, on October 8, 2015, Volkswagen U.S. CEO Michael Horn told the U.S. Congress that it would take years to repair all the cars.

On October 25, 2016, U.S. district court judge Charles Breyer approved a $14.7 billion settlement with Volkswagen. Volkswagen agreed to mail notifications to all affected owners informing them of a $10 billion buyback program, allowing them to turn in their car for cash. In January 2017, Volkswagen pleaded guilty to criminal charges but blamed lower-level engineers for the deceptive software. By 2019, the cost to VW for fines, penalties, restitution, and the settlement of lawsuits exceeded $30 billion. Researchers have estimated that the excess pollution produced between 2008 and 2015 by vehicles equipped with the VW software will create numerous deaths in the United States related to the devices. Adding in effects on health, research published in the journal *Environmental Pollution* estimated that the fraudulent emissions would be associated with 45,000 disability-adjusted life years (DALYs) due to the NOx emitted by Volkswagen vehicles with fraudulent systems. DALYs are a common metric for estimating lost years of life and lower quality of life resulting from ill health or disability. As with its history of killing innocent people in the Nazi era, Volkswagen had again been linked to a shockingly large number of deaths.[11]

On May 3, 2018, former VW CEO Winterkorn was charged in the United States with fraud and conspiracy. The indictment unsealed claims that he was not only fully briefed about what his engineers were up to, but he also authorized a continuing cover-up. Winterkorn's former mentor, Ferdinand Piëch, told German prosecutors that he discussed Volkswagen's software manipulation with Winterkorn. Winterkorn and other senior executives continue to deny that they knew about the fraud, which has important legal implications in the United States, Germany, and elsewhere.

The *New York Times* interviewed a longtime former senior Volkswagen executive who argued that an emissions scandal was all but inevitable at Volkswagen due to the "deep-rooted hostility to environmental regulations among its engineers."[12] The same executive went on to say, "There's no other company where the owners and the unions are working so closely together as Volkswagen. . . . The government and the unions all want . . . full employment, and the more jobs, the better. Volkswagen is seen as having a national mission to provide employment to the German people. That's behind the push to be No. 1 in the world. They'll look the other way about anything."

Illegal action was so central to VW that Audi continued to use the same illegal devices even after the emissions scandal broke in 2015. In 2017, German regulators finally forced another recall at Audi. "We won't make it without a few dirty tricks," a member of Audi's diesel motor development department said in January 2018.[13] In July 2019, German prosecutors charged Audi CEO Rupert Stadler with fraud for his role in the emissions scandal.

One of the amazing and frustrating issues of this story is that Winterkorn and other executives have used their alleged ignorance to fight prosecution and prison. I am not a lawyer, and this book is not about the law. But I do not believe Winterkorn's claims of ignorance. The evidence suggests he was directly responsible for killing many people. Even if I'm wrong about that, when an executive creates an environment that pressures a large number of subordinates to engage in criminal behavior, and when that executive is involved in covering up a crime, he becomes morally responsible for the actions—even if he was technically ignorant. We let too many executives off the hook when we accept ignorance as an excuse from those whose actions lead others to predictably engage in criminal action.

BEYOND THERANOS AND VW

Winterkorn reminds me a great deal of Joseph Ratzinger and Joe Paterno. Before becoming Pope Benedict XVI, while serving as an influential leader in the Vatican's College of Cardinals, Ratzinger was deeply involved in covering up the massive child abuse scandal that occurred within the Catholic Church. Ratzinger, who had access to dozens of reports of child abuse, directed the church to issue denials in the face of strong evidence and to rotate priests guilty of assault from one parish to another, where their sexual assaults could be predicted to continue.[14] Paterno was the legendary longtime football coach at Penn State who, over the course of many years, failed to act on clear information that one of his assistant coaches had been sexually assaulting minors on a regular basis.[15] When leaders create and perpetuate an environment where unethical actions can be predicted to occur, they are choosing actions that make the world a far worse place, and they are guilty of allowing the moral infractions that follow. In such cases, it is an immoral choice not to notice.

Ratzinger and Paterno were not alone in their failure to act on child abuse. Across the most visible recent scandals, large numbers of people typically failed to act. Take the case of Larry Nassar, the Michigan State University physician who sexually abused more than one hundred young female athletes over the course of decades. Ample evidence has emerged that the FBI, the U.S. Olympic Committee, USA Gymnastics, and Michigan State University failed to notice or act despite ample complaints and other signals. These organizations "prioritized their own reputation" over the safety and health of the young athletes, according to a 2019 congressional report.[16]

We are responsible for destroying value when we do not notice the illegal and unethical actions of others and create environments that allow such behavior to persist. There are evil people in the world who seem not to care if they hurt others. They often continue this behavior unchecked because others don't notice, even in the face of glaring evidence. Often, we fail to notice unethical behavior because we are focused too narrowly on what is best for our organization: the Catholic Church for Ratzinger, Penn State for Paterno, VW for Winterkorn. As we saw in Chapter 2 in the discussion about Peter Singer's story of the child drowning in a pond, we also tend not to notice the struggles of people who aren't in our tribe. While we would jump into a pond to save a drowning toddler, we routinely fail to take simple actions that would save the lives of many more people outside our tribe, such as donating money for measles or malaria prevention in distant lands. These are not excuses for not noticing, but a description of the flawed and all-too-common human cognition patterns that need to be overcome.

In his novella *The Actual*, Saul Bellow, the famous fiction writer, created a character named Harry Trellman, who is described as a "first-class noticer." Inspired by this description, the leadership writer and expert Warren Bennis asserts that the most important leadership attribute is to be a first-class noticer, and I agree![17] First-class noticers see opportunities that others miss, are less likely to be blinded by how they want the data to be, and are more open to what the data actually suggests. Perhaps most important, first-class noticers see problems in the environment, including ethical problems created by bad actors or the culture in which they work. First-class noticers are suspicious of things that don't make sense and data that is too good to be true.

I want to push you to be a first-class noticer, just like I try to push myself to be one. Being a first-class noticer requires paying attention to hints that many others miss. It means not limiting your analysis to the data that people give you and instead asking for the data that would most directly respond to the challenge in front of you. It means not accepting solutions that seem too good to be true (as was the case with Madoff's returns, VW's "clean diesel" engine, and Theranos's claims about its technology). And it means searching for more information when something looks suspicious or unclear rather than deferring to others.

PART II

Points of Leverage

CHAPTER 6

REDUCING TRIBALISM AND INCREASING EQUALITY

We like people from our own tribe. We like other people from our own family, neighborhood, school, ethnicity, city, or country. These preferences happen with intention, and they also happen even when we don't deliberate about whom we like, hire, or hang out with. Many years ago, when the first of many studies came out showing that African Americans were discriminated against in the U.S. mortgage market, psychologist David Messick wrote a wise editorial arguing that the primary problem was not that white loan officers were overtly hostile to African Americans, but rather that white loan officers had a positive bias toward people who were a lot like themselves.[1] Clearly, overt racism and sexism persist in our society. Hostility toward outgroups is real, and African Americans have faced far more of the harm of intentional discrimination than other groups. But Messick's observation is consistent with a wealth of social psychological research showing that, today, in-group favoritism may be more pervasive than overt racism and just as harmful. Moreover, I believe readers of this book are much more likely to be biased by in-group favoritism than out-group hostility. And lack of hostility to out-groups doesn't make us immune to tribal behaviors that indirectly harm out-groups.

One of the intriguing paradoxes of tribal behavior is that when powerful majority groups succumb to in-group favoritism (and, by definition, discriminate against out-group members), they often focus on the good they're doing for in-group members. The harm they inflict on out-group members fades from attention. When those in the majority, or in power, give limited funds to people who are like themselves (based on religion, school, nation, etc.), there are less funds available for those who are different from them, including minority groups, women, and the powerless. When we choose recipients for our philanthropy based on their similarity to us, we constrain our ability to do the most good. And when we give limited and coveted spots in universities, corporations, and other exclusive groups to people who are like us, there is less room for diversity.

In his 2013 book, *Moral Tribes,* Joshua Greene describes how tribal behaviors can become a barrier to doing the most good possible.[2] As Greene explains, there's an evolutionary logic to why tribal behavior is so intuitive: in hunter/gatherer societies, relying on our local group, or tribe, may have been central to our survival. But an evolutionary logic does not justify tribal behavior in the current era, particularly when tribal behavior leads to sexism, racism, and hiring the wrong people to work for our organizations.

In the past four chapters, we explored four strategies we can use to be better—to reach more fulfilling, more ethical outcomes for ourselves and for the world. In this next section of the book, we will apply these four strategies to identify concrete actions we can take in four domains to create value. The first involves confronting our tribalism head-on and doing what we can to increase equality.

Counter to the media's portrayals (and often our intuition) of societal woes, psychologist Steven Pinker convincingly argues in his 2018 book, *Enlightenment Now: The Case for Reason, Science, Humanism, and Progress,* that the world is in a much better state today than it has been in the past.[3] Pinker attributes this progress to dramatic improvements in our ability to reason, in science, and in the humanism that developed in the Enlightenment era. Pinker also gives considerable thought to the barriers that are preventing reason, science, and humanism from creating even greater improvements in societal well-being. Perhaps surprisingly to many, but consistent with substantial liberal thought on the topic, Pinker highlights one set of groups as creating barriers to enlightenment: extreme religious groups.

Pinker argues that religious groups that view members of their own group as superior to nonmembers, whether based on their religious beliefs, ethnicity, or nationality, move us away from equality and humanitarian behavior. While religiosity is positively correlated with giving to the poor, Pinker argues that encouragement to give more value to members than nonmembers is one of the greatest barriers to creating even more good. In the process of aiding their members, such religions sometimes end up punishing nonbelievers by not providing them with the help they need, allowing them to suffer, and spreading the view that disbelief in their specific faith will keep nonbelievers out of heaven.

In 2015 in the United States, 33 percent of all charitable dollars went to religious-based organizations. Some religious-based organizations offer donors, implicitly or explicitly, a perception that other philanthropies can't match—a stairway to heaven. Many churches codify this stairway by offering members guidelines on what percentage of their salary they should give to the church.

While some religions recommend a specified percentage of income be donated to their church, few religions recommend giving a specific percentage of their income to a charity other than itself.

Some religious groups explicitly encourage their members to favor their own group and its members rather than people who are in most need of help. In the 2018 Netflix biopic *Come Sunday*, Carlton Pearson, the first African American Pentecostal bishop of a megachurch in Tulsa, lost his church when he changed his beliefs. Pearson was horrified by the 1990 Rwandan civil war, in which 800,000 mostly innocent people were murdered. According to Pearson's religion, since few of these people had accepted Jesus Christ as their savior, most were going to hell. Unable to accept this idea, Pearson rejected the Pentecostal doctrine. He remained a person of faith but started to preach a modernized message of acceptance and inclusion. Pearson's unwillingness to preach Pentecostal principles that defined the criteria for admission to heaven, rather than hell, led to his excommunication from a religion in which he had been a star.

Many people are attracted to religion because they hope to create value in the world. Yet many religions require followers to believe in ideas that may well detract from doing the most good that they can do. Organizations that endorse in-group favoritism, use scare tactics to keep members from using reason, create highly authoritarian structures, and question core findings well accepted by science may not be the strong positive social force that they claim to aspire to be.

AFFIRMATIVE ACTION FOR THE RICH

I belong to an organization that likes and shows a clear bias toward its members. That organization is Harvard University. Harvard's preference for those connected to Harvard emerged in glaring detail in a recent lawsuit. In 2018, Harvard found itself defending its admissions policies in a federal district court in Boston against plaintiffs who accused the university of discriminating against Asian Americans, specifically by holding Asian Americans to higher admissions standards and using quotas to limit their numbers. Filed in 2014, the lawsuit is a recent chapter in a decades-long argument about whether Harvard imposes quotas limiting the percentage or number of Asian American students. (I do not believe that Harvard imposes formal quotas, but that belief is not core to the story I'm telling here.) The case was fairly unique in that the plaintiffs argued that one minority group was discriminated against in favor of whites and other minority groups.[4]

One strategy Harvard uses to discriminate against Asian Americans, the plaintiffs claimed, is to include a subjective personal rating as part of its applicant review process. The lawyers for the Asian American plaintiffs argued that the university uses the personal rating to assess "fit," which refers to the degree to which applicants are similar to the existing tribe—rich white people from families that have been attending Harvard for generations. The plaintiffs connected the use of personal ratings to Harvard's well-documented history of using some notion of "character and fitness" to keep Jews out of Harvard in the 1920s. In 1922, Harvard's Committee on Admissions rejected Harvard president A. Lawrence Lowell's proposed 15 percent upper limit on Jews. There is evidence that Lowell disliked Jews, and he expressed concern that Protestant alumni wouldn't want their children to be around too many Jews. Four years later, when Lowell was still president, the "character and fitness" admissions criterion was adopted. These days, Lowell's anti-Semitism and broader racism have triggered debates about whether his name and image should remain ubiquitous across campus.

The plaintiffs' expert witness in the Harvard case, Dr. Peter Arcidiacono of Duke University, argued that the "personal ratings" given to Asian American applicants lowered their chances of admission to Harvard. Harvard's expert witness, University of California, Berkeley professor David Card, argued that when those personal ratings and other criteria regarding special status (legacy, donor admits) are accounted for, a statistical analysis shows no support for the plaintiffs' claim of discrimination against Asians.

The case was complicated by the fact that the plaintiffs were led by Edward Blum, a white anti–affirmative action activist who broadly opposes special treatment for minority groups. Many of Blum's critics have claimed he used the rejected Asian American plaintiffs as pawns in his war against affirmative action for other minorities, such as African Americans and Latinos. All of the other Ivy League colleges supported Harvard's argument that a loss for Harvard would be a blow to diversity and inclusion efforts throughout higher education and beyond. On October 1, 2019, Blum and the other plaintiffs lost their battle: a federal judge rejected their claim that Harvard had intentionally discriminated against Asian Americans. The judge, Allison D. Burroughs, defended Harvard's use of affirmative action and said the school had met constitutional standards for factoring race into its admissions decisions.[5]

While affirmative action is strongly rooted in arguments around justice, utilitarians have used their own logic to strongly support affirmative action.[6] Utilitarians argue that discrimination harms those being discriminated against far more than it benefits the recipients of favorable treatment. In addition, they argue, discrimination based on inherited attributes is an inefficient means of doling out resources, as they are unlikely to go to those who would benefit most from them. As Mahzarin Banaji, whom you met in Chapter 2, has noted, if you know your steering wheel is biased toward a particular direction, the best way to offset the bias is to pull the steering wheel in the opposite direction.

My hope that Harvard could maintain its ability to create a diverse and inclusive community led me to be on Harvard's side in this lawsuit. Affirmative action allows Harvard to reward applicants who have excelled under difficult circumstances, and I found Blum's exploitive use of Asian Americans insincere, given his broader objectives. My concern about fostering a diverse and inclusive student body is quite consistent with the goal of creating better overall outcomes for society, I believe. However, I'm not happy about all we learned about Harvard throughout the litigation process.

The lawsuit forced Harvard to reveal many details of its admissions policies, many of which are discriminatory, elitist, and far from optimal or ethical. The plaintiffs' discovery unmasked the enormous favoritism Harvard provides to children of Harvard alumni, as well as to people who are willing to make large donations.[7] And, for historic reasons, the majority of Harvard alumni and donors are Caucasian. The magnitude of the benefit accrued from being affiliated with the Harvard tribe is huge: Arcidiacono's expert report claims that Harvard applicants with at least one parent who graduated from Harvard or Radcliffe (Harvard's sister school for women through the twentieth century) were accepted 34 percent of the time, in comparison to just 5.9 percent of non-"legacies."[8] A Harvard analysis found that legacy status conferred a much larger advantage to the most desirable 20 or 30 percent of the applicant pool. Thus, legacy status is unlikely to make up for being in the lower half of the applicant pool, but it helps applicants tremendously at the margin.

Harvard and other elite American schools that admit to favoring legacy applicants claim that they use legacy status as they use race or other student characteristics, to foster a diverse campus—where "diversity" is defined as including people with and without a deep connection to Harvard.[9] Harvard has also argued that legacy consideration "helps to cement strong bonds between the university and its alumni."[10] In addition, Harvard and other schools often claim that alumni donations allow them to financially support the neediest Harvard students. Legacy "applications tend to be well put-together," Harvard's president, Lawrence Bacow, says. "They have deep knowledge of the institution. So, it's a self-selected pool, which, as a group, by almost any metric, looks very, very good relative to the broader applicant pool."[11] While I believe Bacow, I see little reason to give the already-privileged children of wealthy alumni another bonus on top of what their family has already provided them.

Making this case more strongly, Harvard class of 1989 graduate Evan Mandery, who teaches at John Jay College in New York, argues, "There's no plausible moral claim that accidents of birth that advantage you—like being a man, or being a white man, or being a rich, white man—should give you a *further* advantage." Other critics of legacy admissions practices argue that it is unethical for an organization with such a public purpose as Harvard's to discriminate against people who aren't part of the tribe in order to keep the tribe happy.[12] A secondary effect of legacy preferences is to favor the demographic category that is best represented among the alumni population—whites.

It is possible to run a fine university based on merit. Five of the world's arguably top ten universities explicitly reject the idea of legacy preferences in admissions decisions: the Massachusetts Institute of Technology, Caltech, Oxford, Cambridge, and the University of California, Berkeley.[13] But legacy preferences remain strong at many universities, including the publicly supported University of Virginia.[14]

Harvard administrators who want to help people affiliated with

Harvard are thinking about the value they can bring, in terms of building a loyal community and fundraising. They're probably not thinking much about the value they are destroying when rejecting the better-qualified applicants who would have taken these legacies' places. As we've discussed, when people discriminate, it is often because they're focused on helping their tribe rather than on harming outsiders. But when resources are limited, and those who are demographically similar to powerful decision makers get the resource, tribalism, bias, and discrimination are the end result. In college admissions, tribalism creates injustice, destroys the rights of other applicants to be evaluated fairly, and creates a homogeneous culture that misses opportunities to help craft a better society. Helping other people is generally a virtue, but when that help comes cloaked in tribalism, it becomes a vice that needs to be corrected.

The wealthy benefit not just from institutionalized tribalism, but from their ability to further use their in-group status and connections to bias the admissions process. In 2019, federal officials charged more than thirty wealthy parents, including famous actresses Felicity Huffman and Lori Loughlin, with being part of a multimillion-dollar scheme to buy their children into college. These parents allegedly paid a consultant to fabricate academic and athletic credentials and bribe their way into the college of their choice. The consultant, William Rick Singer, engaged in illegal acts to get the children of these alleged criminals into Yale, Stanford, and the University of Southern California. Meanwhile, in 2019, Harvard's longtime fencing coach, Peter Brand, was alleged to have sold a house with an assessed value of $549,300 for $989,500 to a wealthy businessman, Jie "Jack" Zhao. Without living in the house, Zhao then resold the house for $665,000 as the market was appreciating. After the purchase, Zhao's son gained admission to Harvard and joined the fencing team. Now, just to be clear, such actions, if they occurred, differ from Harvard's legacy admission process in that they are illegal. But the broader issue of the inequality created by these various activities, and the past willingness of universities to allow such practices, damages any university's aspirations of being a meritocracy.

I believe that most university officials have good intentions. Yet it is very disturbing to me that these racist, elitist policies remain so widespread. Which begs the obvious question: Why did it take so long for an uproar to emerge regarding unethical admissions policies at our leading universities? Part of the answer is that the harms these policies cause are ambiguous and hard to notice. Erosion of meritocracy occurs incrementally as universities make room for legacy admits. In addition, the qualified applicants who are disadvantaged by these policies rarely complain. While they may be upset about being rejected by a particular school, they don't know that they were rejected in favor of marginally qualified or unqualified legacy admits, nor do we. Imagine if universities had to make public the names of students who would have been accepted if less-qualified legacy admits, or applicants favored by the fencing coach, hadn't taken their spots. Transparency would make the disgrace of legacy admission policies clear and salient to all. The rejected students and the media would complain, the public would be indignant, and the system would have to change.

When the elite are highly overrepresented by one ethnic group, elitism turns into indirect racism as well. A decade or two from now, we will look back and be stunned that the leading U.S. universities would continue elitist and racist policies into the twenty-first century. These policies were developed when society accepted that the privileged were more entitled than others to attend schools such as Yale, Princeton, and Harvard. Such policies implicitly existed from the formation of these elite universities, and more formal legacy admissions policies were created in the early 1900s to keep the most prominent minorities of the time, Jews and Catholics, off campus.

WHERE DOES OUR TRIBALISM COME FROM?

I opened this book by asking you to buy into what may have seemed to be some pretty innocuous ideas, including the notion of equality for all. But, quite honestly, that was a trap—very, very few of us are capable of selecting friends, hiring people, promoting people, and interacting with strangers without being affected by their demographics. And once we're affected by their demographics, equality is no longer possible. This phenomenon is well understood in social psychology, but also in sociobiology and evolutionary psychology.

Sociobiology, a field of study originating in E. O. Wilson's 1975 landmark book on the topic, attempts to explain and examine social behavior within evolutionary principles. More specifically, the field argues that social behavior has resulted from evolution.[15] A closely related field, evolutionary psychology, seeks to identify which aspects of psychological behavior were optimally evolved adaptations—that is, functional for natural selection. Evolutionary psychologists define "optimally" very differently than economists and behavioral decision researchers like Daniel Kahneman do. Critical of the work described in Chapter 2 on decision biases, evolutionary scholars argue that while these patterns of cognition and behavior may not be rational economically, they may be "biologically rational"—that is, suited for the perpetuation of the species. The goal that many evolutionary researchers set for human behavior is not rationality, but rather reproductive fitness. That is, our evolutionarily created responses may have helped steer us away from behaviors encouraged by economic rationality in favor of responses that were biologically rational.[16]

Consistent with Herbert Simon's view that rationality is bounded in part by our cognitive limitations and time constraints, the biological view considers some of our cognitive biases to be the best possible solution to a problem, given the computational and time limitations that people faced many generations earlier.[17] For example, decision-making research on self-control argues that while people *should* maximize their utility, aggregated over time, they tend to err by giving too much weight to present desires and concerns relative to future needs. This lack of self-control can lead to all kinds of shortsighted decisions, from overeating to failing to save adequately for retirement. Evolutionary psychologists argue that such behaviors made sense for our ancestors, who risked dying of starvation if they passed on the short-term rewards of food consumption in anticipation of a larger bounty.[18]

Economists would argue that they do value survival of the species and reproduction, but that these are two of a larger number of goals associated with maximizing utility, including current enjoyment, accomplishing career goals, and making the world a better place. More broadly, just because a behavior was biologically fit many generations ago in a hunter-gatherer society is no reason to accept these suboptimal tilts in our current-day behavior, when we have the option to engage our System 2 processes to maximize our value creation for ourselves and others. In fact, many biologically based behaviors that assured human survival now threaten to sabotage us, as in the case of the energy extraction that exacerbates climate change or overfishing that triggers international conflicts and the depletion of our oceans.

I've covered three perspectives on optimal human decision making in this book: economic rationality, utilitarianism, and reproductive fitness. Evolution may have fostered System 1 decision making that doesn't steer us toward economically rational outcomes in the modern world. As we move the goal from maximizing individual utility (economic rationality) to the ethical goal of utilitarianism (maximizing value impartially—that is, across all sentient beings), we again encounter a conflict between what evolution led us to do and what would create the most aggregate benefit.[19]

Wilson's *Sociobiology* and Singer's *The Expanding Circle* highlight the biological fitness of cooperating with your tribe, even if that means working against your more myopically defined self-interest.[20] That is, those who cooperate with their tribe, such as their family or employer, sometimes make personal sacrifices for the benefit of the group, and as a whole, all members of the tribe are better off as a result of these actions. Moreover, people who belong to cooperative tribes are more likely to survive and reproduce than those in less cooperative tribes. Thus, cooperating within your tribe is biologically fit behavior and may well explain why today we generally care more about ourselves, our family, and other members of a relatively well-defined group that is smaller than the human species. Returning to our discussion in Chapter 3, we can broadly think of this as cooperating in a multi-round prisoner's dilemma problem. The same principles of evolution can explain why we don't make similar sacrifices for out-group members: because there is no biological advantage to doing so. I agree with sociobiologists and evolutionary psychologists who believe this may partially account for why we value and reward our tribe more than those who are far more distant.

But we aren't limited to the intuitive rules of thumb that we have developed over generations: we have the power to engage in System 2 thinking. For many of us, our System 2 thought processes steer us toward equality for all, toward valuing the pain of all people equally, toward impartiality, and toward justice. Consistent with utilitarianism, this means that if we can do great good for those far removed from our group, that is a more ethical action than doing a lesser amount of good for our tribe. This utilitarian North Star often runs up against our evolutionary impulses and System 1 thinking.

IMPLICIT TRIBALISM

The most important discovery about tribalism may be that it often occurs without any intent to preference one group over another. The contemporary literature on ordinary prejudice, led by Mahzarin Banaji and Anthony Greenwald, argues that those who have the power to distribute resources often *implicitly* favor their group over others without being aware of their favoritism or preferences.[21] Implicit psychology shows that we have attitudes about men versus women, whites versus blacks, and, often, "our group" versus "their group." Banaji and Greenwald use the word "ordinary" to clarify that the regular thought processes that we use to categorize, perceive, and judge information can lead to systematic preferences for groups to which we belong. Banaji and Greenwald, along with Brian Nosek, have developed a series of tests that confront people with their tribalism, tests that people have now taken tens of millions of times (to take one yourself, visit www.implicit.harvard.edu).

As a result of our implicit tribalism, many of us frequently fail to treat people outside our tribe with the respect and dignity we show members of our own tribe, or with the dignity and respect needed to create as much good as we can. In her book *The Person You Mean to Be: How Good People Fight Bias,* my colleague and friend

Dolly Chugh builds on the implicit psychology literature to describe how and why well-intentioned people who believe in diversity and inclusion (whom Dolly calls "believers") still miss many opportunities to treat people with the level of equality to which we aspire. As a result, good people fail to create as much value as they could. Chugh encourages all of us to go beyond believing that equality is appropriate to being "builders" who proactively undertake actions aimed at treating all people with dignity and respect. She pushes us to take responsibility for our mistakes and oversights so that we can overcome our limitations and move toward equality.[22]

For me, perhaps the most compelling story Chugh tells in her inspiring work concerns the very simple act of learning someone's name. When meeting new people, most of us are pretty good at recognizing and absorbing the names of members of our own tribe. Yet, in our more diverse world, we often regularly engage with people from other tribes. As a teacher, I have the wonderful opportunity to engage with students from around the globe on a regular basis. I most typically teach groups of MBA or executive students in classes ranging from sixty to ninety-five students. The good news is that Harvard Business School arranges for all students to have a nameplate in front of them during class, which reduces the burden on me and other teachers to remember student names. However, it doesn't solve the challenge of pronouncing those names correctly. Because I don't like the feeling of mispronouncing someone's name, I have tended to skirt this challenge (as, Dolly notes, many of us do) by using the Americanized nickname provided on the student's name card or pointing at people with challenging (to me) names rather than attempting to say their names correctly. A year ago, if you asked me why I didn't at least try to pronounce a student's name, I would have said that I didn't want to offend the student with a mispronunciation. But, to be honest, I was avoiding the work that would be required to learn to pronounce students' names before the course started.

Thus, it was a bit startling for me to read some pretty obvious facts that Dolly highlights in her book. First, people care about their identity, and their names are part of that identity. Second, most names are actually not that hard to pronounce if you take an extra thirty to forty seconds to focus on them; many "difficult" names are simply the aggregation of many easy-to-pronounce syllables. Third, most students would prefer a teacher's sincere attempt to pronounce their name, even with an American accent, as compared to the teacher's obvious attempt to avoid saying their name. Many of us repeatedly fail to step up to this simple pronunciation challenge, instead imposing what feels like a minor cost by pointing. Yet once we take the perspective of the student with the five-syllable "difficult" name, we would easily recognize the wiser strategies of asking them to help us pronounce their name or giving it a sincere try on our own.

I am trying to handle the name challenge more effectively, and the cost is small. For me, Dolly's focus on the use of someone's name highlights one of the many potentially hurtful micro-behaviors we engage in when a bit more reflection would guide us toward behaviors that would create more value in the world. I believe that if I keep Dolly's advice in mind, it becomes easier to act with less tribalism and greater equality.

TOWARD EQUALITY—THE OPPOSITE OF TRIBALISM

It is pretty easy to get liberals and progressive politicians to be in favor of equality, even equality for all. Yet, with the exception of overt nationalists, it is rare for politicians to vocally criticize people for supporting their in-group, even when such action creates inequality. Treating our commitments to our churches, communities, and families as a moral virtue, we rarely stop to consider whether the actions we undertake as a result of these commitments are also creating inequality. Harvard and other elite universities favor not only the children of alumni and donors in their admissions policies, but also the children of faculty. I have lots of liberal professor friends at Harvard (which is located in what is often described as "The People's Republic of Cambridge") who strongly believe in equality for all, yet would never question Harvard's decision to give the children of faculty an admissions advantage.

While most of us readily agree that equality is good, it is far different to act on equality or even to be clear about what it means to be equal. When we say that we believe everyone is equal, what do we mean? Clearly, people have different levels of intelligence; some people are better musicians, accountants, or athletes than others; men are taller than women, on average; and so on. Sexists, racists, and opponents of equality use such facts to argue against the notion of equality as a goal, saying that equality is not an accurate description of the world as it is.[23] Moreover, affirmative-action activists certainly have no interest in ensuring that all job applicants are treated equally; rather, they want those who have been discriminated against in the past to receive affirmative remedies. Yet, as we've seen, equality has long been a part of discussions of ethics and is core to utilitarianism. So, what do we mean when we say that we want equality?

Utilitarians view everyone's *interests* as equal, with interests being defined as maximizing pleasure and minimizing pain. ("Equality of interests" is similar to the use of the term "equity" in many contemporary diversity training programs.) This means that no group's interests should be valued more than those of other groups; the pain and pleasure of all humans should be weighed equally. This doesn't mean treating everyone the same, argues Singer.[24] He gives the example of the aftermath of an earthquake where limited morphine is available to alleviate the pain of the survivors. Should the morphine be divided equally across all those who are suffering or distributed based on patients' level of need? Singer (and I) argue for allocating the morphine based on how it can do the most good. The interests of all are weighed equally, but this doesn't translate into equal treatment or equal division of the morphine. And, while it may seem obvious, it's important to note that the concept of equality of interests is a prescription, not a description of the world as it currently exists.

Even if we accept the idea that the interests of all people should be treated equally, tribalism can threaten our willingness to follow through. Biological and social factors pressure us to do more to try to alleviate the pain experienced by our family members, and perhaps those in our community, city, or country, than the pain of outsiders. While many can agree that the pain of Americans of African ancestry should be as important to address as that of Americans of European ancestry, few of us do as much to address the pain of people in distant lands as we do to help family members who are suffering. Equality of interests is an abstract idea, and it is certainly hard to assess the interests of all. It is also easy to imagine (but not condone) well-intentioned people over-weighting the interests of people similar to them because they understand their interests better than the interests of out-group members. By examining how we diverge from the standard of equality of interests, we can become better and move in the direction of creating more aggregate value.

PUSHING THE LIMITS OF EQUALITY OF
INTERESTS TO INCLUDE ANIMALS

As I argued for focusing on equality of interests, rather than equality of treatment, I violated the very concept of equality of interests by focusing only on humans. What about other animals?

In 1789, Jeremy Bentham, the founder of utilitarianism, wrote:

> *The day may come, when the rest of the animal creation may acquire those rights which never could have been withholden from them but by the hand of tyranny. The French have already discovered that the blackness of skin is no reason why a human being should be abandoned without redress to the caprice of a tormentor. It may come one day to be recognized, that the number of legs, the villosity of the skin . . . are reasons equally insufficient for abandoning a sensitive being to the same fate. What else is it that should trace the insuperable line? Is it the faculty of reason, or perhaps, the faculty for discourse? . . . the question is not, Can they reason? nor, Can they talk? but, Can they suffer?* [25]

Racists create less good in the world by giving greater weight to the interests of some races over the interests of other races. Speciesists create less good than they have the potential to create by ignoring the interests of nonhuman sentient beings. Of course, we are all speciesists, since even the most committed utilitarian favors sentient animals over nonsentient plants. There's a valid basis for this favoritism; nonsentient plants are not capable of suffering or experiencing joy, so they have no interests that need to be considered. Similarly, I have a preference for people and other mammals over insects, which generally have shorter lives and experience less physical and mental pain and pleasure than people and other mammals do.

Arguably, there are a number of good reasons to value humans over nonhuman animals. Due to our longevity and cognition, humans are likely to have more opportunities to experience pleasure than nonhuman animals. We also likely have greater capacity to suffer mental anguish than most nonhuman animals; for example, most nonhuman animals with cancer will suffer the physical downsides but not the mental anguish of fearing or knowing they will die. Yet the argument that most people have more capacity for pleasure and pain should not reduce our concern for the interests of nonhuman animals. Most of us can do more good by placing a greater value on nonhuman animal interests than we currently do, whether by consuming less meat, advocating against the abuse of animals on factory farms, or protecting wildlife habitats.

THE LIMITS TO ACHIEVING EQUALITY

The burden of living up to the standard of looking beyond our tribes to treat the interests of all equally is enormous. We often fail to notice our cognitive limitations, the wise trades where we can reduce our tribalism and get better results, and the corruption that encourages tribalism. But, like you, I know that I can be better and move in the direction of greater equality. I can identify where I fall short and consider adjusting my behavior. I can also think about ways that I can continue to move toward greater equality over time, even as I recognize my current limitations. To use Dolly Chugh's language, I can move from believing in equality to being a builder of greater equality. I hope that you see similar opportunities for yourself.

CHAPTER 7

IDENTIFYING AND ELIMINATING WASTE

In early September 2017, Amazon announced a competition among North American cities and regions to house the company's second headquarters (HQ2). Amazon estimated that the "winner" would gain 50,000 jobs—a tempting prize. All told, 238 cities and regions hired high-priced consultants, developed offers full of costly perks for Amazon, wrote extensive and expensive proposals, and entered the competition. The proposals included amazing amounts of data about the cities, from demographic information to infrastructure plans to zoning codes, and many offered tax incentives, in some cases more than $2 billion. The mere cost of bidding was well into the millions of dollars. By January 2018, Amazon had shrunk the list of contenders to twenty finalists, and in November 2018 announced that it would split its second headquarters between Crystal City, a suburban neighborhood near Washington, D.C., and Long Island City, in Queens, New York. Reportedly,

New York offered Amazon $1.7 billion in incentives, while Virginia and Arlington County offered $573 million.

Many critics have asked whether Amazon truly needed thirteen months and 238 bidders to arrive at the conclusion that it wanted to be located in New York and D.C., especially since it already had a significant presence in both places. Was Amazon's competition nothing more than a charade aimed at generating publicity, collecting data on North American cities and regions to use in future projects, and driving up what New York and D.C. would pay? Even if there were five to ten real contenders, was there any reason to bother the other 200-plus bidders? Or did Amazon lead most of these cities and states to waste enormous amounts of time and money pursuing a dream where they had no chance of success? And for the winning bidders, was it worth $2 billion in subsidies to land HQ2?

The answers to these questions are clear. Amazon led cities and states to waste enormous amounts of money, time, and effort—money, time, and effort that could have been used to improve roads, schools, and health care in the "losing" communities. Amazon may well have benefited by having a third, fourth, and fifth bidder in the race to extract more money from New York and D.C., but the bottom 200-plus bidders added nothing to the company's strategic ability to extract more dollars from the winning bidders. Moreover, any positive publicity the contest generated early on was likely canceled out by the criticism and ill will the company faced in the press and from the losing contestants.

Waste destroys value and makes society worse off. Amazon's contest may have been legal, but it was far from value-enhancing. Waste—from the most normal kind, like buying products that you never use, to the type of wide-ranging, destructive waste created by companies and governments—is one of the key areas where we can apply what we've learned in earlier chapters to great effect for ourselves and the world.

DYSFUNCTIONAL SUBSIDIES FOR CORPORATIONS

Why are U.S. cities and states spending billions of dollars to compete with each other for jobs? Part of the answer is that states independently raise taxes for their own use. In addition, state-level politicians are elected by citizens of just their state and thus have little motivation to cooperate with other states. Many cities and states are also swayed by economists who have argued that tech firms raise wages and quality of life for all. However, a London School of Economics working paper by Tom Kemeny and Taner Osman found that tech jobs reduce real wages in cities because, for those working outside the tech sector, cost of living, including rent, rises faster than wages.[1]

Many in New York and D.C. viewed landing new Amazon headquarters as a victory—certainly, the politicians did. But at a cost of over $40,000 per job ($2.2 billion in combined tax subsidies divided by 50,000 jobs), was this a better investment than using the $2.2 billion on other, more critical community needs, such as schools, health care, housing, and other forms of job creation? Not to mention, when we add in the fact that many of the Amazon jobs would have gone to people who would have moved to the region from other locations, the cost per job for local residents rose far beyond $40,000.

In early 2018, more than six months before Amazon announced its decision, New York University professor Scott Galloway called the competition a "ruse" and a "con," and predicted that the company would decide to locate HQ2 in either New York or Washington,

D.C.[2] Noting that its proximity to both Amazon CEO Jeff Bezos's home and the capital made the D.C. area an obvious choice, Galloway said that "the game was over before it started": it was clear to him that Amazon solicited bids from places it would never seriously consider to drive up tax breaks. Amazon's decision to pick *both* New York and D.C. made Galloway look even more prescient than he would have hoped. While Galloway's arguments can't be proved, plenty of evidence suggests that the competition created by Amazon and perpetuated by cities, states, and Congress contributed to billions of taxpayer dollars being wasted.

This assessment would hold even if Amazon followed through on its agreement—but it didn't. The effort and money New York spent to lure Amazon was a short-lived victory that soon turned to waste. New York's bid and subsequent selection brought out predictable protests. Newly elected New York congresswoman Alexandria Ocasio-Cortez was among those who opposed the deal based on the tax breaks and grants Amazon would have received. While Siena College released a poll showing that 58 percent of registered New York City voters backed the deal, on February 14, 2019, Amazon announced that it was withdrawing from its New York offer, stating that it requires "positive, collaborative relationships with state and local elected officials who will be supportive over the long-term." Amazon further argued that "a number of state and local politicians have made it clear that they oppose our presence and will not work with us to build the type of relationships that are required to go forward with the project."[3] Amazon didn't try to renegotiate or resolve the conflict—it simply walked away. While a minority of New Yorkers celebrated the cancellation, many suffered the costs of being involved in such a wasteful adventure.

In a typical year, American cities and states spend tens of billions on tax breaks and cash grants to urge companies to move across state lines. In the last decade, Boeing, Ford, General Motors, Intel, Nike, Nissan, Royal Dutch Shell, and Tesla have each received subsidy packages worth over $1 billion to either move their headquarters or keep their headquarters from moving.[4] In some cases, this is money that the "winning" bidder may not have needed to spend. Consider that New Jersey and Maryland reportedly offered $7 billion for HQ2, yet Amazon went with New York and D.C., where it already had a strong presence, based on more fundamental business-related criteria. In December 2019, less than a year after bowing out of New York, Amazon announced it was renting office space in Midtown Manhattan for more than 1,500 workers despite not having received financial incentives from the city or state. It was just a fraction of the 25,000 jobs Amazon had promised for Queens, to be sure, but the retailer was expected to continue expanding its footprint in the city over time—all without taxpayer subsidies.[5]

Perhaps the strangest version of this waste of taxpayer dollars is the "Border War" between Kansas and Missouri. For readers who don't remember their U.S. geography, Kansas City, Missouri, lies very close to the border of these two states, with workers regularly commuting from one state to the other. In 2011, Kansas enticed AMC Entertainment to move across the border from Missouri with tens of millions of dollars in incentives. Soon after, Missouri retaliated by offering Applebee's $12.5 million in incentives to move five miles east (and, with no long-term commitment in place, in 2015, Applebee's moved again, to California!). In their competition for jobs and tax revenues, Kansas and Missouri have spent over $500 million luring companies across their border. No net new jobs have been created, but employees have faced problems such as longer commutes, upheaval, and the expense of moving.

Public funding of sports stadiums for privately held teams is another enormous waste of taxpayers' money. This unfortunate trend began in 1953, when Milwaukee lured the Boston Braves Major League Baseball team with the offer of a new, publicly funded stadium. In 1959, the Braves were sold and relocated to Atlanta after the city paid $18 million to build the team a new stadium. For decades, by pitting cities against each other, owners of sports teams have persuaded civic leaders to pony up billions for renovations or new stadiums. The New York Yankees' new stadium, completed in 2009, cost an estimated $2.5 billion, nearly $1.7 billion of which was financed by tax-exempt municipal bonds issued by the city of New York.[6]

The form of funding used by the city of New York, tax-exempt municipal bonds, is noteworthy. Not only would New York owe the principal and interest on the $1.7 billion, but the bondholders would not pay taxes on the revenue from the bonds, thus costing the federal government an estimated $431 million. Consequently, American citizens across the country are paying for the construction of Yankee Stadium. While $431 million is the leader for pro sports stadiums, federal subsidies were also provided to the Chicago Bears' Soldier Field ($205 million), the New York Mets' Citi Field ($185 million), and the Cincinnati Bengals' Paul Brown Stadium ($164 million), among many others.[7] Since 2000, federal taxpayers have lost $3.2 billion in sports stadiums subsidies from the use of tax-exempt municipal bonds, according to a Brookings Institution report.[8]

You might be thinking that the companies involved in this dysfunctional competition, and even the cities, regions, and states, are simply acting rationally. After all, a new sports team could revitalize a city. But there is little evidence that stadiums provide net benefit to local economies, the Brookings Institution argues. And there is certainly no clear economic justification for federal subsidies going to profit-making sports stadiums. Overall, taxpayers are providing corporate welfare to the very rich owners of corporations and sports teams.

Why do cities and states contribute to this waste? Politicians typically act like heroes when they land the new headquarters or stadium, and citizens feel like winners. This happens because they tend to focus on the short-term benefit of "winning" and ignore the opportunity costs inflicted on the community (lost funding for schools, hospitals, etc.) and long-term costs (debt). The common tendency of failing to make a wise trade-off by overly discounting the future for short-term benefits (at the expense of long-term benefits) makes the mistake all the more likely.

Beyond this short-term focus, three additional ingredients contribute to this type of waste.[9]

Social Dilemmas

In Chapter 3, I explained why someone would defect (choose the selfish rather than the cooperative option) in the prisoner's dilemma game and noted that defection generally destroys value. Competition among cities, regions, and states within the United States for companies and sports teams is often more of a multi-party social dilemma than a two-party prisoner's dilemma. If each city or state acts in its own self-interest in competing for the team, all of the cities and states end up with the same suboptimal result, one in which all taxpayers involved provide welfare to the owners of well-off, for-profit corporations.

This pattern illustrates the "tragedy of the commons," a phenomenon documented by ecologist Garrett Hardin. Imagine a group of herdsmen who graze their cattle in a common pasture. Each herdsman would gain a short-term advantage from defecting on the other herdsmen by increasing the size of his herd and grazing the herd on the common pasture. But if too many herdsmen allow their animals to graze, the pasture eventually will be destroyed. The herdsmen are each better off grazing more cattle, but they are collectively better off limiting the total population of cattle to a sustainable level.[10] Similarly, each locality vying to host Amazon's HQ2 might appear to benefit from being the winner, but when they all compete and drive up the cost of winning, they all lose in the long run from the depleted public resources.

Want versus Should Conflicts

When municipalities compete for a sports team, their leaders often understand that they should instead spend their limited resources on schools, bridges, and hospitals. But like the smoker who wants another hit of an addictive substance, yet knows he should abstain to clear his lungs and live a longer life, municipalities too often pay attention to their short-term wants. Politicians benefit from meeting their constituents' immediate desires and rarely suffer personally from pushing long-term debt onto the next generation. As is true for all of us, our wants too often dominate our shoulds, resulting in a pattern of destructive competition.

The Winner's Curse

Imagine that you are competing in an auction against many bidders for a prize whose value is highly uncertain. Not surprisingly, the bidders have very different ideas about what the prize is worth. The "good" news is that you win the auction. Should you be happy? Ample research documents that you should not. When an item of uncertain value is being auctioned, the winning bidder is likely to overestimate the prize's value in comparison to other bidders.[11] This phenomenon is known as the winner's curse. Bidders typically fail to recognize that the party who most overestimates the value of the prize is most likely to be the "winning" bidder.

Now let's consider the case of cities estimating the value of a football team. As long as there is some uncertainty about its value, which there is likely to be, they could under- or overestimate its true value. The "winning" city is most likely to be the one with the most overly optimistic estimate of the team's value. As a result, the winning bidder in such a highly uncertain auction with many bidders typically will pay more than the prize is worth.[12]

Defecting from the common good, overweighting what we want versus what we should do, and the winner's curse account for much of the dysfunctional competition that occurs when governments compete. What can be done? Addressing the simplistic American assumption that competition is always good may be a smart place to start. The goal of the 1957 Treaty of Rome, which created the European Economic Community (EEC), was to create an efficient competitive environment. Article 92 of the treaty defined four core freedoms across member countries—movement, capital, services, and goods—and declared that any aid granted by a specific country that distorts or threatens to distort competition within the community violates the treaty. The article served to limit dysfunctional competition across countries and promote efficient competition. By contrast, although U.S. states have a country in common, the American tendency to defer to states' rights, combined with a naïve view of the unilateral benefits of competition, allows states to engage in dysfunctional competition with each other and creates enormous waste.

"We need a national truce, both within states and between states," Amy Liu, the director of the Metropolitan Policy Program at the Brookings Institution, argues. "There should be no more poaching of private companies with public funds."[13] Clearly, to adequately address this problem, the federal government would need to make changes aimed at preventing dysfunctional behavior at the state and municipal levels. One option would be for Congress to ban interstate competition, much as the 1957 Treaty of Rome did among European nations. If banning sounds overly restrictive, Congress could tax state or local incentives as a special kind of income, effectively taking away their benefits, as the recipient organization would have to pay whatever it gained to the federal government. Such a federal tax would motivate cities to change their development strategies to create new value rather than inefficiently stealing value from other cities.

Waste in the Food System

On New Year's Day, 2019, I attended a vegan luncheon of the Boston Vegetarian Society with Rachel Atcheson. I had met Rachel in passing through other events connected to effective altruism and reducing animal suffering, but did not know her well. Rachel, who is in her late twenties, majored in philosophy at Boston University. She is a committed effective altruist and a central actor in the movement to reduce animal suffering. She previously worked for the Humane League and now works as deputy strategist for Eric Adams, the borough president of Brooklyn, New York. Her job is to position Brooklyn as a leader and advocate for health and wellness, with the not-so-hidden secondary objective of saving more animals by changing the eating habits of New York residents and visitors. Rachel is a nice, passionate activist. She is proud of her past dumpster diving, an activity aimed at reducing (or some might say consuming) waste by rescuing food discarded by restaurants.

The Boston Vegetarian Society met that day at a very good vegan restaurant called Grasshopper in the Allston neighborhood of Boston. There were about ten tables of eight in the restaurant for the sold-out seating of this private group. At our table of eight, large amounts of food were served family style, and there was much more of it than we could possibly eat, though I did my best. Consistent with the society's waste-reduction values, at the end of the meal, the restaurant passed out takeout containers so that attendees could pack up some leftovers. Knowing that Marla, my spouse, had already planned to cook dinner that evening, I passed on taking any of the food home (otherwise, I would have been happy to do so). Rachel pleasantly made sure that her table companions had all they wanted, then made it clear she wasn't going to let the leftovers go to waste. She filled four quart-sized containers full of food, including food from the table next to ours, and started thinking about which of her friends she'd share the abundance with that evening.

Rachel did this without conveying greediness, but rather a passion for keeping food from going to waste. Waste moves us away from value creation. The episode clearly captured an aspect of how Rachel leads her life, where veganism, utilitarianism, and waste reduction come together nicely. I admire Rachel, even if I don't aim to match her lifestyle. I walked away from lunch with lots of insights about our shared interests, such as emerging plant-based food products, but my main impression from the lunch was watching someone truly strive to be better by reducing food waste.

Food waste is an enormous problem, and one that nice people contribute to without giving it much thought. And there is so much we can do. When so many people remain hungry—not just across the globe, but in our own communities—we should be bothered by the fact that nearly half of all food produced is wasted. When most of us think about food waste, we think about the uneaten food on our plate at the end of a meal.[14] But there's much more to it than that. Food waste is exacerbated by impulse buying, the large portions served in restaurants, spoilage, failing to consume food before it expires, and viewing buffets as "eat-as-much-as-you-can" rather than "eat-as-much-as-you-desire."

For every one garbage can of waste you put out on the curb, seventy garbage cans of waste were made upstream just to make the waste in that one garbage can you put out on the curb.[15] The world's annual catch of fish and marine invertebrates is approximately 100 million metric tons, but only 20 percent is processed for food use. Approximately 30 percent of that 20 percent (we are now down to 6 percent) is consumed, and the rest is discarded as waste. Many species of fish and invertebrates are rarely used as food because they possess an undesirable flavor, color, or size.[16]

Fifty percent of U.S. land is used to produce food, and 30 percent of our energy resources are used to process the food. Yet farmers often throw away a third or more of their harvest simply because it fails to meet the public's cosmetic standards. This produce is "discarded, perfectly edible, because [it's] the wrong shape or size," notes Tristram Stuart.[17] Part of this waste is caused by Americans' distorted notions of what a high-quality product should look like. Ugly, delicious heirloom tomatoes have only become desirable in the last decade; nearly tasteless, mass-produced tomatoes have been the norm in large part because they look good. We lose food during processing and transportation, and by overstocking the produce and meat sections of the supermarket. The blogger Harish, who specializes in quantifying information about the animal advocacy movement, notes:

> Most vegans and vegetarians would agree that no animal should have to suffer or die for our food. But, even most omnivores would agree that there is something deeply wretched about inflicting lifelong pain and misery and finally death on an animal for food we are not going to eat.[18]

Many project a dramatic shortage of food as the world population grows to 9–10 billion by the middle of the century, with protein expected to be in particularly short supply. This is in part because the calories needed to feed animals amount to anywhere from four to a hundred times the calories that humans consume from the animal products.

More than any other food, beef highlights both the waste humans create and the opportunities that are available to reduce waste. I am sure you already know that beef isn't good for you and is correlated with many of the worst diseases that threaten your life span. Worldwide, cows require 100 times the calorie input of the calories that they will eventually provide to humans, and 25 times as much protein as they will provide.[19] (In the United States, due to the efficiency of the beef industry, these ratios are 40:1 and 16:1, respectively.)

Most animals and animal products are wasteful, but beef is an extreme case. The good news is that there are plans in place to create a less wasteful food system. A combination of health factors, environmental consideration, efficiency, and concerns about animal suffering have led to a dramatic growth in plant-based products, including meat substitutes—about 20 percent growth per year.[20] All indications are that this growth will continue in the future. More dramatically, as we discussed in Chapter 1, the Good Food Movement is focused on creating new, better-tasting plant-based products, as well as "cultivated meat" (also called "clean meat," "cell-based meat," and "cultured meat"), a new technology that cultivates the tissue of an actual animal to produce meat without needing to feed, torture, or kill an animal. All of these advances waste far fewer calories and protein than conventional meat produced by killing an animal. The first cultivated meat burger was produced in 2013, and reasonably priced clean-meat products are five to fifteen years away.

There are nonprofit organizations that are encouraging the development of new plant-based and clean-meat products, such as the Good Food Institute. In addition, a growing number of venture capital organizations and famous entrepreneurs (including names like Gates, Branson, Brin, and Welch) see this industry as a potentially lucrative investment opportunity. Some of you may already be tired of my animal rights views, but one interesting aspect of the Good Food Movement is that its leaders, like Bruce Friedrich of the Good Food Institute, have broadened their focus from just encouraging people to be vegetarian or vegan, to also shifting the balance of the foods consumed by flexitarians, reducetarians, and others. Getting people to eat in a more sustainable way requires the creation of great new products—ones that meat eaters will be happy to eat based on superior taste, cost, and convenience, in comparison to food that comes from ending the life of a sentient being.

One unique aspect of the venture capital world's interest in good foods is their collaboration. In many industries, competing venture capital funds only coordinate when they invest in the same entrepreneurial venture. In the good foods world, many of the venture capitalists involved are vegan, and part of their focus is on reducing animal suffering and food waste. As a result of this social mission, they are coordinating to bring as many new products to market as possible. One vehicle for this coordination is the Glasswall Syndicate, which describes itself as a "large group (over 150) of venture capitalists, foundations, trusts, non-profits, and individual investors who share a similar investment thesis and want to accelerate mainstream adoption of products and services that will make a difference in the lives of animals [and] people, and that are better for the planet."[21] Glasswall members (I am one of them) invest in start-up plant-based and cultivated-meat companies, and actually root for entrepreneurs who are developing meat alternatives, even when they aren't investing in the specific start-up.

If you think the market for good foods is limited, you might consider that Tyson Foods has invested in cultivated meat start-up Memphis Meats. Tyson currently produces about one-fifth of the chicken, beef, and pork in the United States. Tyson CEO and president Tom Hayes acknowledged that the investment "might seem counterintuitive," but he explained that in a world with a growing population in need of protein, Tyson will have to figure out how to answer these demands in a sustainable way. Tyson previously invested in the plant-based meat alternative Beyond Meat.[22] If the good food industry proves successful, Tyson wants to be at the table with access to new technology for creating the protein that consumers demand.

Of course, consumer-created waste goes well beyond food. More than half (58 percent) of the total energy produced in the United States is wasted due to other inefficiencies, such as wasted heat from power plants, vehicles, and lightbulbs.[23] We can typically reduce such waste without making any personal sacrifice at all—in fact, our greater efficiency will save us money while making the world a slightly better place.

PARASITIC INTERMEDIARIES IN THE NONPROFIT WORLD

Imagine that your phone rings while you're having dinner. You answer it, and the person on the other end tells you a moving story about some people in need of your financial help. We have all received such calls, and many of us have made donations. Clearly, my view is that you will make better charitable decisions when you aren't considering just one organization over the telephone while wanting to get back to dinner. In fact, there is a very good chance that if you do make a donation, the money will be wasted.

When we give money over the phone, we are generally responding to an emotional appeal. This emotional appeal is exploited by parasitic intermediaries who work for profit-making organizations to scam people out of their money. A shockingly large amount of that money goes to the intermediary, and very little of it serves those who need help. One example is Help the Vets, a nationwide operation that solicits donations to fund veterans' medical care, including breast cancer treatment, a suicide prevention program, and retreats for those recuperating from stress. Help the Vets makes emotional pleas to potential donors to help veterans, such as noting that for those who served in Iraq and Afghanistan, "giving an arm and a leg isn't simply a figure of speech—it's a harsh reality."[24] The organization sounds as if it has the best of intentions, yet Federal Trade Commission chairman Joe Simons writes that evidence shows that Help the Vets, from 2014 to 2017, "spent more than 95 percent [of its incoming donations] paying its founder, fundraisers and expenses."[25]

Many charities hire intermediaries, primarily telemarketing firms, to do their fundraising. Given that no one likes telephone solicitations, why does it remain such a common fundraising tool? For-profit companies know they can make money by taking on a task that not many charities enjoy. According to the National Center for Charitable Statistics (NCCS), more than 1.5 million non-profit organizations are registered in the United States, twice as many as there were twenty years ago.[26] (That's too many; more on that below.) As these organizations compete for charitable dollars, professional solicitors manage to convince them that they are burdened with delivering services. In addition, they offer the charity money that seems to be a bonus on top of what they would earn if they tried to raise funds themselves. So, the charity accepts the intermediary's offer of a small portion of the actual money that is raised. The charity focuses on its mission and ignores the fact that donors' limited charitable dollars are being squandered. By paying employees low wages, the intermediaries make a bunch of money—often as much as 75 percent of what they raise. This process is technically legal, but it's highly unethical. When people are tricked into believing that their money is primarily going to those who need it, but it's actually profiting an organization not even mentioned in the sales pitch, it becomes clear that money is being wasted and that we need a better way to donate. Charities that participate in this process allow the intermediaries to create a wasteful enterprise that shrinks the overall charitable pie and manipulates uninformed contributors.

"If every charity reduced its fund-raising expenditures," Janet Greenlee and Teresa Gordon note, "all would benefit from higher net proceeds; [but] if only one charity reduced its expenditures, the remaining charities would reap the benefits."[27] If all charities eliminated the use of such intermediaries, collectively, they would raise more money. When nonprofits hire such intermediaries, they are defecting in a social dilemma, reducing the amount of productive charitable dollars available to all groups. Nonprofits should see that the collective good requires them to say no to intermediaries that funnel profits for themselves. Because attempts to regulate the profit margins of professional fundraisers have been struck down by the courts, a more viable plan may be to continue to increase the transparency of charities' spending habits.[28]

Parasitic intermediaries aren't the only source of waste in the nonprofit world. *Boston Globe* reporter Sacha Pfeiffer (a member of the Pulitzer Prize–winning team of reporters that exposed the Catholic Church's cover-up of clergy sex abuse) tells the story of OneGoal, a nonprofit whose mission is to help disadvantaged students graduate from college.[29] Pfeiffer argues that the problem with this new nonprofit is that it has the same goal as more than forty other Boston nonprofits. This duplication of effort adds up to waste: money spent unnecessarily on office space, operational inefficiencies, and staff competing for the same charitable contributions. It means time and money wasted on writing forty year-end reports, filing forty tax returns with the government, and having

forty different fundraising efforts, often targeted at the same donors. In the for-profit sector, this type of inefficiency would lead
some competing organizations to fail and go out of business and
others to merge, but those market forces are not fully available
for nonprofits. "One thing I see over and over again is duplication
of effort—so many small organizations that are doing the same
work or very similar work," Marla Felcher (full disclosure: I am
married to Marla), the founder of a women's collective giving organization, the Philanthropy Connection, told Pfeiffer. "People
say, 'Oh, my nonprofit is different than that one,' but if you're on
the outside, you don't see the difference. . . . I think some of our
smaller organizations would be best served by working more
closely with or becoming part of a larger, better-established organization." In the nonprofit world, waste adds up to solving fewer
of the world's problems.

In my industry, academia, there is a consistent and widespread
need for more space. Many universities and colleges hold back
on hiring new staff members, faculty, or visiting scholars not because they can't afford to pay them, but because they don't have
enough offices available. Yet professors are often busy people who
spend a lot of time outside of their offices. In addition, we refer
to our bookshelves less and less as our world works in more dig-
itized ways. Professors can and often do meet with others, check
email, and write from home, cafes, libraries, and other remote
locations. As a result, it is common for the majority of faculty offices to be empty even during the middle of the day in the middle
of the semester. So, if we don't use our offices fully, why don't we
share them? Other professionals who also work outside of their
office a great deal, such as consultants, have moved toward "ho-
teling" (shared workspace) arrangements. Unfortunately, professors seem to accrue prestige based on their office, with wasted
space and missed opportunities as the result.

THE WASTE WE CREATE

How did you ever acquire all of that stuff in your basement, garage, or attic? Too often, we make purchases based on our emotional response to them rather than on whether we will want to own them a short time later. We also often confuse waste reduction with negative judgments like "being cheap." If we want to create more value, we should strive to see waste reduction as a useful way to make the world a bit better, while perhaps saving some resources along the way—moving toward that Pareto-efficient frontier depicted in Chapter 3.

There are many actions we can take to create less waste, and each of us is likely to see different opportunities. Some of us might think about the added fuel we use by driving an inefficient car, or driving when other means of travel are easily available. Some of us can do a better job of thinking ahead when we are about to make an impulse purchase. And some of us could buy a bit less food so that less ends up in the trash. But, overall, our willingness to confront our waste is likely to pave the way to value creation. In the next chapter, we will look at one of the most crucial assets that we waste—our time.

CHAPTER 8

ALLOCATING YOUR MOST PRECIOUS ASSET—YOUR TIME

What are you most short of in life?

What is your most critical resource?

Many of us quickly offer the same answer to these two questions: time. But lots of research evidence shows that many of us also make mistakes when allocating our time. Consider the following problem:

> *Imagine that you are about to purchase a printer cartridge in a store for $50. The salesperson informs you that the cartridge you wish to buy is on sale at the store's other branch, located a 20-minute drive away. You have decided to buy the cartridge today and will either buy it at the current store or drive 20 minutes to the other store. What is the minimum discount that you would require at the other store such that you would be willing to travel there for the discount?*[1]

Implicitly assessing the value of their time, many people argue that the obvious answer is to assess the trade-off between the time they would save versus the money they would save. It is common for people to demand a $20 to $30 savings to drive twenty minutes for the discount, and almost all respondents would make the twenty-minute drive if they could save $40 off the $50 price.

Now consider the following related problem:

Imagine that you are about to purchase a computer for $2,000. The salesperson informs you that this computer is on sale at the store's other branch, located a 20-minute drive from where you are now. You have decided to buy the computer today and will either buy it at the current store or drive to the store a 20-minute drive away. What is the minimum discount that you would require at the other store such that you would be willing to travel there for the discount?

In both cases, you face a simple trade-off of time versus money.[2] How much money is required to make the trade-off worthwhile? Yet, when researchers compare how people respond to these two questions, they find that most demand a much larger discount in absolute dollars in the computer trip than in the cartridge trip. It is common for people to pass on a $60 discount on the computer if it means a twenty-minute drive, yet quickly decide to make the same drive to get a $40 discount on the cartridge.

Why the inconsistency? When we think about "getting a good deal," part of our assessment is guided by the percentage discount we are receiving. This focus on getting a good deal can lead us to waste time, assuming our goal is to save the most amount of money possible for the time we invest.

Tversky and Kahneman wrote the initial version of this problem, and I've always found it fascinating.[3] This is in part due to my own misallocation of my time throughout my life. Quite honestly,

I could easily be guilty of passing on the $60 computer discount, yet going for the $40 cartridge discount simply because I couldn't pass up an 80 percent discount. I am also mildly obsessed with getting a good deal on my airfares and hotels, to the point where I am sure that I am saving far less money than I think my time is worth as I obsessively search the internet for a better deal.

With this awareness in mind, around my fiftieth birthday, I thought it would be useful to think a bit more systematically about how I use my time. I already knew that in terms of work/ life balance, I am heavily tilted toward work, in comparison to most people and the recommendations most people would make for others. I work hard, and I work long hours. Generally speaking, though, I love my work, so that is okay with me. I enjoy teaching. I enjoy advising. I enjoy conducting research. I enjoy "having written" (more than the moment-by-moment writing itself). And I enjoy my outside consulting work (and have done a pretty good job of turning down outside work that I thought would not be fun or impactful, even if it meant passing on a profitable opportunity).

But it's also true that I certainly don't enjoy every moment of my working life. So I decided to review what aspects of my work I don't fully enjoy and the adjustments I might make. One conclusion I reached was that I don't enjoy attending faculty meetings. Fortunately, it's also true that my presence at them often adds little value. Sometimes I think my input is helpful, and I am happy to provide it. But—like many of you, I'm sure—I also have walked out of many meetings after an hour or two, thinking that there were would have been far better ways for me to use my time. So I started to pass on attending certain faculty meetings where I didn't feel I would add much value. (I do realize, and appreciate, that I am in a fortunate point in my working life where I can skip faculty meetings without suffering any severe career consequences.)

Another task that is part of being a good academic citizen is serving as a "peer reviewer" of papers submitted to academic journals in one's field. Given the large number of submissions that academic journals receive, they require a great deal of peer reviews. It is typical for journals to have an editorial board consisting of better-known scholars, who are expected to review more papers than other reviewers. There is some prestige associated with being asked to serve on an editorial board. However, most social science journals do not pay editorial board members and other reviewers for this work; it is something that we are expected to do as good citizens in our academic community. (Some academics, including me, are annoyed that we do not get paid, as the corporate entities that run the journals charge excessively high fees for subscriptions to their journals.) As an editorial board member, you are expected to read a broad range of papers, and some inevitably are quite distant from your own interests. Many of the papers I was being asked to read were not ones I would have taken the time to read if I weren't on the editorial board. And by the age of fifty, I had reviewed enough papers in my lifetime that I doubted I was bringing the same enthusiasm to the task that an advanced doctoral student or younger faculty member might provide. Thus, it wasn't clear that anyone was getting sufficient benefit for the costs I was incurring. I was even more firmly convinced that I could be a better academic citizen by devoting the hours I was spending reviewing papers to other tasks that interested me more. So I quit the four editorial boards of the journals that sent me the most papers. These were prestigious journals, and some of them were edited by personal friends of mine. I didn't quit to be lazy, but to make the best use of the time I was willing to spend contributing to the broader good.

Referring back to the chart in Chapter 3 that depicts the value we create for ourselves and others, we can see that any amount of time we devote to helping others can be depicted as a move from Point A to Point C. This chapter raises the question of whether you could move to a far more efficient outcome than Point C, to a point that sacrifices the same amount as the move from Point A to Point C but creates far more good for others. I hope that I used some of the time saved from skipping faculty meetings and quitting editorial boards in a constructive manner to create value in this way.

This chapter will help you think about how to use your time more wisely, both for your own benefit and for the benefit of others. I'm not going to lecture you about using your time on more serious matters at the expense of enjoyment: plenty of evidence supports the argument that many people work too hard and play too little. Rather, I hope to encourage you to find ways to maximize your cumulative pleasure and minimize your cumulative pain, and, when you decide to help others, to do as much good as possible with the time you invest.

People tend to spend a lot of time thinking about how to use their limited money but fail to undertake the same type of examination of how they spend their time. I found the exercise of auditing how I spend my time quite useful, and I encourage you to give it a try. You're likely to come to some surprising discoveries that will provide insight into how you can do more good, given your limited time.

TIME VERSUS MONEY

Benjamin Franklin was the first person known to claim that "Time is money."[4] But in our era, at least, we fail to follow the implications of Franklin's advice; that is, we don't make wise trade-offs between time and money. We're used to budgeting (as opposed to scheduling) our money, but not our time.[5] This is true despite the fact that money is more fungible than time: money that you don't spend can be spent tomorrow, but time not used well today is gone forever.

My Harvard Business School colleague Ashley Whillans is an expert on how people make trade-offs between time and money, and how they might do better.[6] Ashley and her colleagues find that while people claim they lack time, their behaviors reflect an intuitive tendency to spend large amounts of time to save relatively small amounts of money. This is consistent with my admission above about spending too much time to save too few dollars when looking for the best airfare and hotel prices. Ashley's research shows that, by contrast, we're happier when we spend money to buy time—that is, when we pay other people to do time-consuming tasks we dislike, whether that is gardening, laundry, cooking, or troubleshooting what's wrong with your computer.

Western culture leads many of us to pay attention to and deliberate over our money, but not our time, Ashley argues. Many of us learn from a young age that people who are important are busy—that is, short on time. Moreover, we are taught to value money more than time. We get monetary bonuses for good performance, but we rarely get time off, or a memo from our boss releasing us from the tasks we like the least or those where we provide the least value (like those faculty meetings I mentioned earlier). As a result, when we defer to our intuitive, System 1 thinking about how to allocate our time, we misuse and run short of time. But when we reflect more deeply on the trade-off between time and money, many of us realize that our behavior doesn't reflect the true value we place on our time. When we move toward more deliberative System 2 thinking, we make better trade-offs between time and money.

In Ashley's recent book, she also argues that guilt keeps us from outsourcing disliked tasks to buy time.[7] That is, we feel bad about paying people to do things that we could do on our own, such as cleaning our house or delivering our groceries, even when we can afford to do so and when willing employees are available to perform these services. She also finds in her research that we don't want others to know that we pay for such services. This thinking is flawed, she concludes: others want the work, and in the process of providing them with employment, we increase our own happiness.

TIME VERSUS TIME

It's time for us to audit how we use our time to do good in the world. We can look at how we might be misallocating time to tasks that we aren't rewarded for and don't enjoy. And we can identify tasks that we should offload to others.

Please begin by listing activities you have engaged in over the last two months where you contributed your time to help others. Here is my partial list:

- I taught a class for a colleague who was ill.
- I attended a nonprofit benefit for an organization whose board my spouse belongs to.
- I read and commented on a colleague's forthcoming book.
- I took our food scraps to a nearby compost pit rather than dumping them in the trash can.
- I attended a conference focused on reducing animal suffering, with the primary goal of learning.
- I attended a boring committee meeting that I expect will generate few concrete outcomes.
- I gave a friend some negotiation advice on securing funding for her new start-up.

- I spoke to multiple people about the academic fields in which I work. Some of the conversations had to do with research, others with teaching.
- At a colleague's request, I gave a talk at a conference in Washington, D.C., without receiving a fee.
- I met with the development director of a charitable organization run by a friend. The nice person I met with was seeking a charitable contribution.

As I review this list, I conclude that most of these items were fine uses of my time. But for a few of them, I would love to get my time back. The Washington, D.C., conference took too much of my time in comparison to the value that I believe I created: the attendees seemed entertained by my talk, rather than (as I'd hoped) inspired or ready to take action in their organizations. Meeting with the development director isn't going to change my charitable giving and served no real purpose other than being polite. The boring committee meeting really didn't require my attendance. In contrast, the compost walk was pleasant, and I combined it with a relaxing dog walk.

I have made a mental note of these observations for the future, and hopefully this type of audit will lead me to continue to strive to make better use of my time. But what I really need (and maybe you do, too) are some more systematic ways of thinking about my future time commitments. Luckily, some are available.

In 1817, the British political economist David Ricardo introduced the economic concept of comparative advantage.[8] At an organizational level, a company has a comparative advantage if it has the ability to sell goods and services at a lower cost than its competitors. This concept helps highlight the advantages of trade, including global trade, as discussed in Chapter 3.

At the individual level, a person has a comparative advantage when she can do a task at a lower opportunity cost than other people. For those new to the term "opportunity cost," think about the best use of the person's time if they didn't work on the task in question. The word "opportunity" highlights the difference between comparative and absolute advantage. Someone who is the best at doing something is said to have an absolute advantage. Thus, consider an evening where my spouse, Marla, and I need to walk the dog and prepare dinner in the next forty minutes. Marla is better at walking the dog than I am (as measured by the happiness of the dog, Becca). But while Marla is a better dog walker, her superiority over me at preparing dinner is even greater. Thus, while I am not the best dog walker in the family, I have a comparative advantage at walking the dog, even though I don't have an absolute advantage. This is due to Marla bettering me at dinner preparation far more than she exceeds my skill as a dog walker.

Marla and I create value through the benefit of comparative advantage beyond the cooking/dog walking example. We both aspire to do good in the world, we both have multiple advanced degrees, and we both work lots of hours per week. But Marla is far more effective than me at advising and appreciating the operational details of nonprofits, is the cofounder of a thriving philanthropy, and writes a blog on resisting corrupt behaviors in our national government (www.marlafelcher.com), activities that do not pay her significant fees. I am more effective at finding opportunities to provide consulting services for high fees, being careful not to take projects that I think will create net harm. The two of us are relatively comfortable with the fact that I make a fine salary, and Marla spends more of her time helping nonprofits directly. Marla also makes most of our charitable giving decisions. Collectively, we are both happier and create more value from this arrangement than we would if we both split our time equally between money-making activities and working directly with nonprofits.

Note that my and Marla's joint decision-making processes depart sharply from simpler notions of fairness, such as "everyone should do half of every task." Far more value can be created by making wise trades across tasks that take advantage of who can do the task more easily, who enjoys the task more, and who can do the task better. Partners don't need to make an explicit trade every time either partner performs a task, but making sure that both parties are aware of the long-term benefits they will receive from making wise trades across tasks and across time seems like pretty good marital advice.

Similarly, imagine that a founder of a technology start-up might be the best person in the firm at completing detailed technical tasks, but only slightly better than the next-most-talented person in the firm. At the same time, the founder might be dramatically more effective than anyone else in the firm at representing the start-up to key strategic partners or investors. Thus, while she has an absolute advantage on the technical side, her comparative advantage does not lie in doing the technical work. The concept of comparative advantage highlights where she can do the firm the most good: by representing it to others.

I am proud of my ability to mentor doctoral students who have many absolute advantages over me—including writing nicer prose, being better at analyzing data, being smarter, and so on. But I also think that I have organized my research groups in my career in ways that benefit from the comparative advantages of different people to create the best research possible. Some of my students have been great project managers, others strong at data analysis, and others amazingly creative idea generators. Engaging our System 2 thinking encourages us to harness the talents of those around us and get the most from our limited time.

Everyone has a comparative advantage. Our time is best spent in areas where we have a comparative advantage rather than an absolute advantage. In contrast, many of us have a propensity to want to do tasks where we have an absolute advantage, even when we do not have a comparative advantage. Wise organizations allocate tasks to employees in ways that allow them to benefit from the comparative advantage that different people bring to different tasks.

The concept of comparative advantage helps us allocate tasks among different people. But there are also times when we must decide whether to allocate our time to a task without knowing who will do it if we don't, or if the task will get done at all. Imagine that, around the same time, you are asked to join a neighborhood improvement committee, serve on the board of a nonprofit, and meet with a friend of a friend who might benefit from your advice. You would like to be helpful, but you do not have enough time to say yes to all of these requests, even if you stay up late. For these tasks, it isn't practical to think about whether you have a comparative advantage. But you could think through how much good the use of your time would create in comparison to other uses of your time. For one or more of these tasks, your analysis may lead you to conclude that you would not create much value and thus to feel just fine about refusing. You aren't saying no because you are selfish, but because there are better ways for you to create value with the scarce resource of your time.

TIME AND DOING THE MOST GOOD

The organization 80,000 Hours (https://80000hours.org/) provides coaching to help young adults (age twenty to thirty-five) find careers that allow them to make a positive social impact. The name of the organization stands for the approximate amount of time they will spend working during their lifetime. If you accept this goal of creating as much value as you can, how would you select your career? Following a rational decision-making process similar to the one I outlined in Chapter 2, 80,000 Hours recommends that you think about some of the most important problems in the world and identify what is keeping society from overcoming them. Now shrink that list to problems where you have the motivation and skills to contribute substantial value. 80,000 Hours then recommends that you take the next step on the highest-impact path, perhaps seeking a job in the chosen career path, while also having a backup plan that allows you to respond as uncertainties in the environment are resolved. Then, periodically (for example, once a year), review your plan and decide whether any adjustments are in order.

Thousands of people have redirected their careers based on 80,000 Hours' career advisory programs, which are particularly popular with undergraduate and graduate students in more technical fields, such as computer science, molecular biology, and applied mathematics. One critical decision facing young professionals is whether to give now, by working and contributing, or to increase their career capital—their expertise and knowledge—by developing the skills, connections, and credentials that could help them make a bigger positive impact in the future. Career capital can come from formal education, working with a great mentor, finding an internship that focuses on developing your skills and interests, and so on. This is often a tough choice, but it's also true that very few people who invest in their future later regret that investment. Realizing that you have 80,000 Hours ahead of you may provide some motivation for taking a long-term perspective.

You might imagine that 80,000 Hours encourages people to spend their 80,000 hours working in the nonprofit world, but that's not necessarily the case. Rather, the organization encourages people to figure out how they can do the most good over their lifetime.

While for some, the answer may be working for a charitable or government organization, for others, it might mean maximizing your income in the for-profit world so that you have more to give away—"earning to give." Another way to make an impact is to entrepreneurially innovate in ways that could make the world better. If you can create a product or service that reduces disease, saves lives, feeds the poorest people in the world, or educates people more effectively, you are creating enormous value. 80,000 Hours also accepts that some people have unusually strong personal career preferences and simply encourages them to continue down that path and contribute more of their earnings. Perhaps the most counterintuitive program connected to 80,000 Hours is Raising for Effective Giving (REG), a nonprofit that collects money for effective charities (more on what I mean by "effective" in the next chapter) from poker players. Participating poker players pledge at least 2 percent of their winnings to charities suggested by REG. REG is currently generating more than $1 million a year for very effective charities from this voluntary taxing of winnings.

While 80,000 Hours focuses on people early in their careers, all of us face the issue of how to best use our time to make the biggest impact. One of the most interesting career shifts I have encountered is the journey of Uma Valeti. Valeti grew up as a meat eater in India and became a vegetarian while in medical school. He earned a cardiology fellowship at the Mayo Clinic; later, in his cardiology practice, he was involved in a study that used stem cells to repair heart muscle tissue damaged in heart attacks. Valeti realized that if stem cells could be used to regrow heart muscle tissue, the same concept could be applied to grow animal muscle tissue, or what most of us call meat. After unsuccessfully trying to convince other scientists to start a company to cultivate animal tissue with the goal of producing (cell-based) meat without killing any additional animals, Valeti quit his job as a cardiologist to start a company to produce cell-based (or "cultivated") meat.

While he believed that he was helping people as a cardiologist, Valeti had a realization: "I might save maybe a few thousand lives over the next thirty years. But if I am successful in helping to change the way meat is made, I could positively impact billions of human lives and trillions of animal lives."[9]

Valeti believes that he can produce tasty products without the need for animals to die and without the negative health effects on humans of eating meat. He envisions using his biological knowledge to cultivate and genetically improve meat in ways that can make it tastier, cheaper, and healthier. Armed with these insights, Valeti founded Memphis Meats, which is now at the forefront of the cultivated meat world, potentially complementing the impact of plant-based companies like Beyond Meat and the Impossible Burger. Memphis Meats quickly attracted an amazing list of investors, including Bill Gates, Richard Branson, and agriculture giants Cargill and Tyson, and recently raised an additional $161 million from investors.

Memphis Meats is a very risky high-tech company that is at the forefront of a food revolution. In the context of our discussion, it's fascinating to learn of a cardiologist who gave up a fruitful career because he saw another path that could create greater good. Here is how Valeti thinks about it:

> I got into cardiology because I wanted to positively impact human health. I see my role at Memphis Meats as an extension of that mission—I get to play a larger role in improving our food system from a public health perspective. The world's population is on track to exceed 9 billion by 2030. Without major innovations, the ever-growing number of mouths to feed could become a catastrophic public health crisis. Our innovation could play an integral role in sustainably feed-

ing the world. In addition, this innovation has huge potential from
an environmental sustainability and animal welfare perspective.[10]

Valeti didn't choose to try to create value by working for a non-profit or donating large amounts of money; rather, he took a far greater risk to try to have a far bigger impact. He made this change with a very capitalistic mindset: if his assessments are correct, he will soon be a very wealthy individual. I hope that he is, because if he gets rich from Memphis Meats, he will create enormous value for the rest of us sentient beings.

Valeti made a tough decision to give up cardiology to try to do the most good he could do. We all frequently face smaller choices regarding how to allocate our time. Should you join the group cleaning litter from the highway? Should you serve on a board of a nonprofit? Or should you work an extra billable half day at a very high hourly wage and donate your earnings to charity? Obviously, these are your choices to make, and any of these options would make the world better. Some people find the earning-to-give strategy to be too far removed from the action of doing good, or even elitist. But 80,000 Hours doesn't share this view.[11] The organization cites Roman historian Sallust, who valued the Roman statesman Cato the Younger because "[h]e preferred to be good, rather than to seem so."[12] According to this view, the successful financial executive who can turn hours into earnings may be able to minimize more suffering than if he helped to clean up the highway on his days off, even if the latter has intuitive appeal to many.

JUST SAY NO—SO YOU CAN DO MORE GOOD!

I have a number of friends in Pittsburgh. I grew up there, received my Ph.D. from Carnegie Mellon University (CMU), and served on multiple external review committees for CMU. I have remained in relatively close contact with a number of professors there. One of my friends in Pittsburgh is Linda Babcock. Linda is the James Walton Professor of Economics and the former acting dean at CMU's Heinz College of Information Systems and Public Policy. Linda and I have never written a paper together, but have been in closely related fields for decades. Linda's 2003 book, *Women Don't Ask: Negotiation and the Gender Divide*, was recognized as one of the seventy-five smartest business books of all time by *Fortune* magazine. One of Linda's colleagues at Carnegie is Laurie Weingart, the Richard M. and Margaret S. Cyert Professor of Organizational Behavior at the Tepper School of Business. Laurie was a doctoral student at the Kellogg Graduate School of Management at Northwestern when I was a professor there in the 1980s. Laurie and I wrote a paper together, I attended her wedding, and I've been friends with her over the last few decades. Laurie has served as a senior associate dean at Tepper and as the interim provost of the university. Very fine scholars, Linda and Laurie are also good people who have been recognized for their citizenship to Carnegie.

In 2010, Linda became overwhelmed with the number of "non-promotable" tasks on her desk. In academia, some of what we do is rewarded (publishing in leading academic journals) and helps us advance in our careers, while other tasks are expected but contribute little to promotions or other tangible rewards (such as serving on lots of committees). As this story develops, it is important to note that Carnegie is a very male-dominated culture, Linda and Laurie are female, and there are many fine people at Carnegie who want women to be represented on visible committees. In addition, both Linda and Laurie are known for getting things done, so they get asked to provide lots of service. And, as Linda has told me, if she says no, it probably means that the administrator seeking to staff a committee will turn to one of Linda's female colleagues to make sure that the committee has female representation. Linda had a hunch that women are asked to accomplish such thankless tasks more often than men and that women, on average, also have more difficulty than men saying no to such requests. So Linda asked four of her colleagues, including Laurie, to meet up for drinks to discuss her theory. They bonded, and the "I Just Can't Say No" club was born.

This group of professors and professionals gathered socially, published research on the topic, and helped each other think more carefully about how they spent their time at work.[13] Their research showed that both men and women expect women to volunteer more readily and that part of the reason for this expectation is that women do, in fact, agree to volunteer more often. In terms of their own time management, while both Linda and Laurie want to contribute to CMU, their professions, and the broader society, given that their time is constrained, saying yes to all the service requests that come their way cannot be the wisest strategy, or even be possible. The "I Just Can't Say No" club provided them with inspiration to reflect and make wise decisions about where time can create the most value. Their research has implications for all of us, including men, who claim that we are short on time and face too many demands: we can treat requests for our time as a prompt to think about whether the requested task is the most effective way for us to do good with the limited time we have available. Linda, Laurie, and I are firmly convinced that women can often do more good as a result of their increased willingness to say no to some things so that they can spend their time in other, more valuable ways. They are currently writing a book on just saying no, along with Lise Vesterlund and Brenda Peysar.

In addition to avoiding faculty meetings, I also avoid meeting with prospective applicants to a variety of graduate school programs at Harvard, whether I'm affiliated with them or not. This sounds harsh, but hear me out. I get more requests from people asking to meet, talk by phone, start research projects, or spend a semester or a year working with me at Harvard than I could ever come close to accepting—even if I stopped writing, conducting research, and so on. In a typical year, I get about forty to fifty requests from people who are in the admissions process for graduate school at Harvard, asking to meet up with me. Many of them have fine reasons to contact me, such as a genuine passion for a topic that I study, or wanting to learn more about a specific program at Harvard. Others simply want to influence anyone at Harvard who will speak with them in the hope that they can positively affect the admissions process. These applicants have no reason to know that, in most cases, I cannot help them: my advice or recommendation typically would have zero effect on the admissions process. And, if I did have influence, meeting with these people would put me in the position of potentially discriminating against people who do not know it is possible to request such a meeting or cannot afford to travel to Cambridge to meet with me. I am confident that people with a number of advantages to start with are most likely to reach out in this manner. So, about ten years ago, I resolved to respond to all such requests by explaining that I have a policy of not meeting or talking with applicants while the admissions process is ongoing. I also tell them that after they know if they have been accepted or rejected by Harvard, I would be happy to talk with them, regardless of whether they might end up at Harvard. I rarely get such follow-up requests. I believe that I use the time saved by my policy more efficiently, which sometimes means spending that time helping others in ways that I find to be more ethical.

HOW SHOULD YOU SPEND THE REST OF YOUR LIFE?

I probably spend more time thinking about how best to use my time than most people do, but the process of researching and writing this chapter has surprised me by highlighting just how important it is to use my time wisely. In particular, I have become fascinated by the degree to which I have misallocated my time in the past. I'm not talking about spending more time enjoying myself rather than working. I'm talking about the time I've allocated to helping others: I've spent time on tasks that I thought would create value, only to recognize later that I could have created much more value for others if I had spent that time differently.

Of course, we need to be careful about applying concepts such as comparative advantage too narrowly. Taken to the extreme, it would be easy to ask why I would ever walk my dog, Becca, when others who value their time at a far lower wage could do it. The simple answer is that I like my dog, I like walking my dog, and I don't want to think about my leisure time in monetary terms on a moment-by-moment basis. Yet, as has been the case for me, reflecting on how you use your time may allow you to identify other tasks that you do not enjoy that others can take on for a price that you would be happy to pay. And you might also identify ways to do more good for others by taking advantage of some of the value-creating moves highlighted in this chapter.

CHAPTER 9

GETTING THE MOST BANG FOR YOUR PHILANTHROPIC BUCK

Immediately after a vivid disaster strikes, the donations appear. When Hurricane Mitch hit Honduras, a plane full of needed supplies couldn't land because of the piles of clothing clogging the runway. The clothing, which included many winter coats, had arrived in a planeload of previous donations. Winter coats in Honduras!

After hearing reports in the news of the latest disaster—whether a hurricane, flood, mass murder, or earthquake—many people are eager to do something to help. Donating clothing or other goods, such as cans of food or diapers, tends to strike us as more personal than simply sending cash. We have an urge to send goods that show those who are suffering that we care about them. But humanitarian workers refer to the crush of useless, often incomprehensible contributions as "the second disaster."[1]

In December 2012, after a gunman killed twenty children and

six adults at the Sandy Hook Elementary School in Newtown, Connecticut, stuff started arriving almost immediately. Newtown employee Chris Kelsey estimated the number of donated teddy bears at 67,000, in addition to thousands of boxes of toys and clothing.[2] "I think a lot of the stuff that came into the warehouse was more for the people that sent it than it was for the people in Newtown," Kelsey remarked. "At least, that's the way it felt at the end."[3] Every child in Newtown got a few teddy bears; the rest had to be sent away, along with most of the other goods sent.

This anecdotal data is consistent with the general argument that cash donations often make more sense—and are much more needed—than teddy bears or winter coats in the aftermath of a disaster. Cash is fungible; it can be spent on whatever's needed and used to relieve suffering virtually anywhere.

But sometimes there's even an abundance of well-meaning cash. In the six and a half years after the Sandy Hook shootings, more than $100 million flowed into the small town of 28,000 people in southern Connecticut, according to the *New York Times*.[4] General Electric, which employed the father of the gunman, paid for a $15 million community center. But to survivors, it was an unpleasant reminder that felt like more of a wound.[5] The money caused conflict in Newtown, did little to address the societal problems that contributed to the shootings, and certainly did not undo the deaths. "The town became a case study of how American material expressions of grief can become more an obstacle than an aid to recovery," the *Times* story concludes.

Large nonprofit organizations often use the vividness of disasters, natural and man-made, to create the emotional tug needed to generate charitable contributions. Such pleas often work, and the donations flood in. We intuitively want to respond in a way that might offer healing, while also creating an emotional connection between us and the victims. But reacting emotionally to the most immediate disaster may not be the best way to spend our charitable dollars. Upon greater reflection, using our System 2 thinking, regardless of whether we donate a little or a great amount, we can recognize more effective ways to help others.

TOWARD MORE EFFECTIVE ALTRUISM

Let's imagine what would happen if you sat down at the end of the year and thought hard about who should receive your charitable dollars in the coming year. (If you already do this, I applaud you.) You might start with some goals or principles that you endorse, based on your personal values. One principle might be to contribute in a way that creates the most good in the world. To do so, you decide your dollars should go to organizations that spend money efficiently and effectively. Your egalitarian instincts also motivate you to want to give your money in a manner that doesn't discriminate against specific groups of people. You may also care about reducing animal and human suffering, consistent with the utilitarian notion of valuing the pain of all sentient beings.

The good news is that there are many organizations that share these goals. In fact, you can find them listed at https://www.give well.org/charities/top-charities. These goals lie at the core of effective altruism, a rapidly growing social movement that seeks to apply evidence and reason to determine the most effective ways to improve the world. Popular books in the effective altruism movement include Peter Singer's *The Most Good You Can Do* and William MacAskill's *Doing Good Better*. Effective altruism pushes us to consider all the consequences of our actions and then make our charitable contributions in the way that is expected to make the greatest positive impact on the world. The movement is rooted in utilitarianism but isn't rigid in its attachment to any specific philosophical perspective; it's simply rooted in the goal of making better, more effective philanthropic decisions. It would be impossible for most of us to assess whether we are effective altruists, since the answer isn't a simple yes or no. But the world would be better off if we tried to be more effectively altruistic when making our charitable decisions.

In contrast to pure utilitarianism, which specifies what you would *optimally* do to make the world a better place, effective altruism instead focuses on being better. Effective altruism guides people in a utilitarian direction without expecting pure utilitarian behavior. This includes encouraging people to donate more than they do currently, to make commitments while they're young to give away more of their income as they become wealthier, and to donate in a way that will have the greatest positive impact on the world. While Peter Singer is clearly the hero of the movement, philosophy is not at its forefront. Effective altruism conferences, which have been held regularly since 2013, attract a very young audience and serve only vegan food. The effective altruism movement is also enthusiastic about harnessing the best scientific evidence available (including the use of randomized control trials) to figure out where contributions can have the greatest impact. Controversially, effective altruists often conclude that donations create much more benefit in poor countries far from the United States and other Western nations. Their priorities also include reducing the suffering of animals in factory farms and leaving the world in good condition for future generations—who, they argue, have equal moral value to currently existing people.

Based on rigorous analyses, effective altruists assert that some charities are far more effective than others, and they seek to identify those that achieve the most good for a given amount of money. Effective altruism assesses impact based on geeky measures such as "quality-adjusted life years" (QALY) saved per dollar.

So, imagine that multiple charities seek to save lives, and you want to know which saves the most lives per dollar contributed. But, of course, some people have more expected years left in their lives, and we also care about the quality of those years. Assessing the QALYs that can be saved by each charity for the same contribution is a logical way to compare their effectiveness—and that is precisely what the effective altruism world pushes us to do.

The effective altruism movement has been led by Oxford philosophers William MacAskill and Toby Ord. They were involved in the creation of the Centre for Effective Altruism at Oxford, which houses 80,000 Hours (discussed in Chapter 8), and Giving What We Can, an organization that encourages people to pledge to donate at least 10 percent of their income for the remainder of their working lives to causes consistent with the effective altruism movement. As of 2019, more than 4,265 individuals have taken the pledge, donating over $125 million. Similarly, the Founders Pledge is a nonprofit that enlists for-profit start-up founders to make a legally binding commitment to donate at least 2 percent of their personal proceeds to charity in the event that they sell their business. By August 2019, 1,205 entrepreneurs had made such a pledge and donated $365 million. Other important organizations in the effective altruism movement include GiveWell and The Life You Can Save, both of which provide scientific guidance on where our money can do the most good. For those focused on reducing animal suffering, Animal Charity Evaluators provides similar analyses.

You don't need to adopt utilitarian philosophy to join the effective altruism movement; nor are you expected to become a perfect utilitarian, as none of us can be. You can simply focus on doing better with your donations.

Despite being a bold new movement, effective altruism remains a small part of the philanthropy world. It is dominated by very young people. Consider one of the heroes of the effective altruism movement, Ian Ross, whom Singer has described as leading "the most remarkable example of a life committed to maximizing giving." Ross earned a Ph.D. in linguistics from the University of Pennsylvania, following undergraduate work at MIT, and currently works for Facebook's product analytics team. Following a strategy that he describes as "earning to give," he has committed his life to reducing extreme animal suffering. Going well beyond the basic tenets of veganism, Ross believes each of us is responsible for what we do and what we do not do, and he applies that logic to how he lives. While working for large corporations, he was a founding advisor to Hampton Creek Foods (rebranded as Just Foods), which produces plant-based egg substitutes that are already reducing the demand for eggs. In 2014, Ross donated more than 95 percent of his $400,000 income after taxes to charities. Living alone in San Francisco, he claimed to have a comfortable lifestyle within an annual budget of $9,000. By 2016, at an effective altruism conference at MIT, he said he was making a bit under $500,000 and living on $10,000, including his monthly rent of $400 per month (yes, in San Francisco!). He may be the most extreme practitioner of the "earning to give" idea discussed in Chapter 8. Sure, he gets mugged occasionally in his low-rent neighborhood, but he views this as a small price to pay on the path to living an effectively altruistic life. Ross does not view his lifestyle as a sacrifice; he believes himself to be simply a vessel for reducing as much animal suffering as possible.

I admire Ian Ross, but I don't aspire to his lifestyle, and I question whether he is an ideal exemplar of effective altruism. Ample evidence from the goal-setting literature suggests that the most effective goals are those that are perceived as challenging, but not impossible or unreasonable. Ian Ross may view his lifestyle as quite pleasant, but others are unlikely to perceive it as possible or reasonable for themselves. Consequently, too many people may reject pure utilitarianism as a guide for their behavior, as it appears to require far too much sacrifice. As an alternative, it would be useful to convince people to broadly buy into the principles underlying utilitarianism, identify the very normal barriers to their willingness to act in a purely utilitarian manner, and then explore which of these barriers they might eliminate to be better.

A SHORTSIGHTED CRITIQUE

A number of watchdog organizations have tasked themselves with evaluating charities' efficiency to help people maximize the impact of their donations. Charity Navigator, for example, shows particular disdain for high overhead. It aims "to advance a more efficient and responsive philanthropic marketplace in which givers and the charities they support work in tandem to overcome our nation's and the world's most persistent challenges."[6]

Many people consider donating to charities to be a very personal task. Some critics have accused the effective altruism movement and watchdog groups like Charity Navigator of being paternalistic—of ignoring the heart and deep emotions that often surround giving while arrogantly claiming to know the "right" way to give. Not surprisingly, these organizations' use of terms like "intelligent giving" can offend people. And, of course, many nonprofit organizations that do not perform well in the eyes of these watchdogs certainly do not appreciate their insights. Effective altruists would counter that while emotions may create the reason to give, they can limit the effectiveness of how we give.

Because effective altruists and charity watchdog groups seem to share the goal of maximizing efficiency in the realm of charitable giving, I was surprised to read an article in the 2013 *Stanford*

Social Innovation Review in which Ken Berger, then the president of Charity Navigator, and Robert M. Penna, a consultant to the organization, viciously attacked effective altruism as "defective altruism." Berger and Penna were offended by effective altruism's goal of assessing what does the most good across charitable domains (for example, education versus hunger), which leads to the assumption that all suffering and pleasure can be compared and measured. Berger and Penna accuse effective altruism of being "a moralistic, hyper-rational, top-down approach to philanthropy" (not much different from criticisms I'd read of Charity Navigator). They also attacked Peter Singer's famous query concerning whether it is better to provide one guide dog to one blind American or to cure two thousand people of blindness in a developing region, if either could be done for the same price. Singer and the effective altruism community clearly believe that the more moral choice is to prevent the two thousand cases of blindness, even if the recipients live far away from donors. By contrast, Berger and Penna believe it's up to donors to decide which societal problems they want to help ameliorate, as long as they choose charities with low overhead. Essentially, Berger and Penna endorse metrics that encourage organizations to spend the vast proportion of their funds on directly providing services or goods, but have no problem with donors picking and choosing among causes and tribes. In accusing effective altruists of rating causes they like over causes they don't like, Berger and Penna convey that either they don't understand or choose to give no credence to the underlying logic of utilitarianism of maximizing the value created by one's philanthropy.

By being the first mover on quantifying charitable organizations, Charity Navigator may have captured the imagination of those who value efficiency in efforts to make the world better. It did so, however, with an overly narrow objective. Research clearly shows that goals, such as identifying charities with low overhead, will motivate people's behavior—in this case, their donation decisions. But it's also true that goals that focus on one set of desired behavior lead people to ignore other desirable behaviors.[7] Thus, Charity Navigator's metrics are likely to lead philanthropists to focus on low-overhead organizations while ignoring more important information: the amount of good their charitable dollars will achieve. Ignoring this other information will keep donors from making even better decisions. By the way, few financial executives would recommend Charity Navigator's low-overhead metric as the sole basis for evaluating business investments. Some of the most profitable corporations in the world invest a lot in R&D and in competitive salaries, and have high overhead rates as a result.

Effective altruism, Charity Navigator, and other movements and organizations that seek to guide charitable donations generally do far more good than bad. Moreover, these organizations can harvest the best of what we have learned in psychology and behavioral economics to nudge people to maximize pleasure and minimize pain. They can help us trade up by making wise trade-offs on the impact that we can have through different paths to charitable giving. But when organizations in the philanthropy community denigrate other positive movements or generous donors, they make philanthropy less attractive as a whole. In attacking the good being done by the effective altruism movement, Charity Navigator destroys value for the world. Its website still provides useful advice, but its leaders' criticism of effective altruism is costly. They could do better.

MY VIEWS ON PHILANTHROPY

Just to be clear, I'm a fan of the efficiency and low overhead promoted by Charity Navigator, as well as effectiveness and the other goals espoused by effective altruists. Here are a few more guidelines I support when it comes to charitable giving:

- PEOPLE HAVE THE RIGHT TO DONATE AS THEY CHOOSE. Since we are talking about voluntary donations rather than tax dollars, we need to accept that people have the right to make the final determination regarding whether and how they donate their funds.
- DELIBERATION LEADS TO WISER DECISIONS THAN INTUITION. Beyond the world of charity, there is ample evidence that people make wiser decisions when they are deliberative rather than when they are following their gut instincts. System 2 thinking leads to wiser decisions than System 1 thinking; in the realm of philanthropy, this translates into greater value creation.
- WELL-ORGANIZED DATA IS EXTREMELY HELPFUL. Because all of us are overwhelmed with information, having it organized in a manner that allows us to better understand the characteristics of different charities and how they compare can be enormously helpful.

EFFECTIVE CHARITIES

Different people reach very different conclusions about which charities are the most appropriate to fund with their philanthropic dollars. Based on their values (outlined earlier in the chapter), effective altruists reach some clear conclusions.[8] They focus on problems that are large in scale (problems that significantly affect many people's lives) and are solvable—that is, where contributions can make a substantial difference. Effective altruists also favor charities that have proved to be effective at saving lives and alleviating suffering (both human and animal). Effective altruists also believe they can have a greater impact on problems that have been neglected. For example, many organizations and philanthropists are paying attention to the important problem of finding a cure for cancer, while malaria is comparatively ignored. Effective altruists thus conclude that our contributions can save more lives when applied to reducing malaria rather than cancer.

In total, these values lead effective altruists to identify three categories of charities where our contributions can alleviate the greatest amount of suffering.

First, charities that focus on fighting extreme poverty in low-income countries have enormous potential to reduce suffering, and there is excellent evidence from the field of developmental economics of the effectiveness of different interventions. There are easily preventable diseases, such as malaria and parasitic worms, that kill millions of people every year. Similarly, poor nutrition in low-income countries leads to a large number of preventable maladies. All of this suffering is relatively easy to prevent. Even simply transferring money to people who are very poor is a relatively cost-effective way of helping them. The philanthropy Give-Directly distributes money straight to those in need, with very little administrative costs in the process. They have already distributed millions of dollars to 20,000 individuals living across 197 villages. Consistent with the values of effective altruism, Give-Directly actively studies the effectiveness of its aid; over time, this allows them to be more effective.

GiveWell—which, as I mentioned earlier, offers hard data on how to make sure our money does the most good—estimates the cost of saving an expected life for many of the charities that they view as most effective. This is the kind of comparative reasoning that pervades the effective altruism community. It leads effective altruists to focus on bed nets over antimalarial drugs, even though antimalarial drugs are more cost-effective than the efforts of virtually all other philanthropic efforts that focus on developing economies.[9]

Second, addressing the type of tribalism we discussed in Chapter 6, many people who identify with the effective altruism community focus on animal welfare, arguing that if we value a unit of animal suffering like we value a unit of human suffering, then we can reduce the greatest amount of suffering by focusing on animal welfare. (This is not the same as arguing that an insect is as important as a human, since humans have more capacity for pain and pleasure than an insect.) Like Givewell, Animal Charity Evaluators (https://animalcharityevaluators.org/) is an online platform that sorts out where your charitable dollars will do the most good, but with a specific focus on animal welfare. As Animal Charity Evaluators notes, billions of animals each year are kept in inhumane conditions on factory farms, and their lives end prematurely when they are slaughtered for food. Animal welfare advocates argue that much of this suffering can be eliminated by reducing demand for factory-farmed meat and by enacting legislative changes that improve the welfare of farmed animals.

At the beginning of this book, I described a lecture by Bruce Friedrich that changed my philanthropy, investments, and consumption substantially. To review, his organization, the Good Food Institute, focuses on encouraging the creation of the next generation of foods that will reduce demand for products that come from abusing and killing animals. While the Good Food Institute is a charity, it is connected to investment groups that fund meat alternatives. Beyond donating to reduce animal suffering, investing in meat alternatives and consuming the products of these efforts are additional or alternative strategies toward creating value.

A final argument for a focus on animals is that they are underserved in the philanthropic community: only 2.8 percent of philanthropic funding in the United States goes toward improving the environment and animal welfare (the other 97 percent is aimed at helping humans). And of that 2.8 percent, the majority is spent to help domesticated and wild animals, despite the greater opportunity to reduce the suffering of animals in factory farms.

Third, effective altruists care not just about current generations, but also about future generations. The number of people who will exist in the future is likely many times greater than the number of people alive today. Effective altruists believe that these people matter and that we should value their future pain and pleasure similarly to our own. Yet we often fail to think about our great-grandchildren, let alone their great-grandchildren. They are too emotionally distant from us to create an emotional tug.

What can we do to cost-effectively improve the welfare of future generations? There are many speculative answers to this question, and given the different scientific interests and expertise of members of the effective altruism movement, people reach different conclusions. But within the scientific community, most scientists would agree that an effective way to improve the welfare of future generations is to pay far more attention to the climate change crisis than we currently do. While this tends to be more a matter of political decision making than charity, there are many charities focused on slowing climate change. The website https://founderspledge.com/ offers a good starting point for thinking about how your dollars can best address climate change. Founders Pledge cites the Coalition for Rainforest Nations and Clean Air Task Force as two charities that are making headway in the fight against climate change.

MOVING BEYOND OUR BARRIERS
TO WISE PHILANTHROPY

Our emotions play a critical role in motivating us to help others, as you doubtless know if you've ever considered donating to a heartfelt GoFundMe plea on Facebook or picking up the phone to give money after seeing photos of suffering dogs and cats in a TV ad. Even if you're convinced by the effective altruism perspective, for the sake of social connectivity, you may be happy to fund your friend's participation in a charity race, though it isn't the most effective form of philanthropy. But it's still important to be aware that our emotions can lead us to get less bang from our philanthropic bucks.

Imagine that you are trying to fundraise for two different charities. The first serves a needed population but does so very ineffectively, spending a great deal on overhead and passing on little to the intended beneficiaries. However, this charity has amazing success stories to share in its promotional materials, and its recipients are identifiable and live near likely donors. The second charity is just the opposite: it scores well in the effective altruism community, creates great value per donated dollar and is highly effective, and focuses on people across a big ocean, and its recipients are not visible to those making donations.

Now imagine that you can send an emotional message (such as a video that highlights the suffering of a specific person) or a rational message (such as data describing the magnitude of good that donated dollars can do) to potential donors on behalf of each charity. Which type of message do you send? If your goal is to raise funds for your organization, research supports focusing on the emotional message if you are the first charity. Lots of philanthropies rely on the strategy of tugging on people's emotions to make up for a less-than-compelling value proposition. In fact, many consultants are thriving thanks to their recognition that people often make charitable decisions based on their emotions.[10] They draw on the same barriers to active intelligence we explored in Chapter 2, including creating a warm glow for the donor, providing them with recognition, and creating connections between donor and recipient. In contrast, if your services are remarkably cost-effective, you'll want people to engage their active intelligence by conveying a cognitive message as well. Basically, if you have great stories but a less compelling value proposition, you want people to act on their emotional response. But the better your value proposition, the more you also want people to be cognitively engaged.

That's the charities' perspective. Now let's return you to the role of a prospective donor who wants to be as impactful as possible with your charitable dollars. You should try to engage your active intelligence by identifying organizations that have made wise trade-offs in what they seek to do with their limited funds and that are honest and transparent.

Here are some specific process recommendations. First, think through your overall goals: What do you want to achieve with your contributions? This step may sound obvious, but many smart people skip it. I've noted that effective altruists lean toward creating as much value as possible by being efficient and effective, and valuing the interests of all equally. But perhaps you want to make some adjustments, based on your rejection of some aspect of utilitarian logic. For example, you might not care about animal suffering as much as human suffering, or you may feel a particular obligation to a tribe to which you belong (such as your religious institution or your alma mater). The remaining utilitarian logic still holds and can be adjusted according to your specific values. I personally make philanthropic decisions with my spouse, and her preferences often depart from the charities most preferred by effective altruists (more on this in Chapter 10). But we do think about the effectiveness of the organizations we consider, have shifted toward more effective charities, and have been on a path of donating a greater percentage of our income over time.

It is also useful to see where your intuition contradicts advice from effective altruism or your own more deliberative analysis. This might mean taking a look at the organizations that have received your donations over the last year and considering why you gave the funds. In retrospect, is this where you would want your donations to go? This gives you a chance to pit your intuitive System 1 preferences against your deliberative System 2 preferences, and update what you truly believe to be a wise philanthropic strategy. After all, your emotive self could have an important message that you feel you need to hear. How should you resolve any discrepancy that emerges? Effective altruism certainly argues for preferencing cognitive over emotional analyses. Not ready to accept this? Perhaps you might benefit from a parallel analysis from one of the greatest decision scientists who ever lived, Howard Raiffa.[11]

According to an often-told story, Raiffa was on the faculty at Columbia when he received an offer from Harvard. So Raiffa met with his dean at Columbia, who was also his friend, and asked for input on what he should do. In an attempt at humor, the dean, borrowing from Raiffa's writings on decision analysis, suggested that Raiffa identify the relevant criteria, weight each criterion, rate each school on each criterion, do the arithmetic, see which school had the best overall score, and go there (a great deal like how effective altruists assess charities). Raiffa purportedly responded, "No, this is a serious decision!" Raiffa, my friend and informal mentor until his passing, clarified to me many times that while he enjoyed the story, it simply isn't true. But Raiffa also argued that when intuition and deliberation clash, it is wise to consider whether your

emotions provide insights that should be part of your more deliberative decision-making process and to use that deliberation to
help you see how your emotions might steer you away from your
long-term goals. In terms of philanthropy, this contrast can also
allow you to audit your decisions for bias that might result from
valuing a warm glow, a desire to be recognized, and allegiance
to your tribe. I think that this is great advice for those who aren't
ready to fully endorse the goals of effective altruism.

To achieve even greater clarity, you could try to think through
what choices you would make under a so-called veil of ignorance—
that is, as if you didn't know your own tribe, wealth, or nationality.[12] Doing so can help reveal how your identity might be biasing
your philanthropic plan.

Finally, you can organize your donations in a manner that increases their effectiveness. Let's look at two common ways of
timing donations. First, many of us receive and consider donation
requests as they appear throughout the year—in the mail, on social media, at church on Sunday, in your child's backpack, and so
on. Second, many of us sit down periodically to think through our
donation patterns across many philanthropies. I admit I use both
of these processes. Yet the evidence is clear and consistent: thinking through our donations across organizations—the type of joint
decision-making process we explored in Chapter 2—better en-
gages our active intelligence, prompts more rational decisions, and
helps us create more value. Sequentially considering charities as
they appear to us throughout the year directs our attention to the
emotional tug of philanthropic appeals, whereas comparing different charities leads to logical deliberation across options. So, let's
all strive to slow down and deliberate when one-off requests show
up in our inbox or mailbox, and also to sit down more regularly to
consider our philanthropic goals and decisions thoughtfully.

This chapter completes our exploration of four domains (equality, waste, time, and philanthropy) where you can consider strategies for creating more value. The final two chapters will focus on developing an action plan for increasing your ability to create value by influencing the decisions of others for good.

PART III

Creating More Value
for You and the World

CHAPTER 10

MULTIPLYING VALUE CREATION THROUGH OTHERS

Many researchers have argued that after people have obtained a moderate level of wealth, additional wealth does not make them any happier. In a very compelling and rigorous study, however, economists Betsey Stevenson and Justin Wolfers disproved this claim, finding that additional wealth does improve happiness, and in a very consistent manner.[1] They find a geometric, rather than arithmetic, relationship in their study of citizens from the twenty-five most populous nations. That is, doubling one's income creates a similar increase in happiness, regardless of whether you are earning $1,000, $10,000, or $100,000 per year. That means that an increase in income from $1,000 to $2,000 annually creates about the same increase in happiness as an increase from $100,000 to $200,000.

Based on Stevenson and Wolfers's study, and Peter Singer's

related writing on the topic, Oxford philosopher William Mac-Askill argues that there's a pretty easy strategy that people with even moderate incomes in developed economies can follow to create more happiness in the world: give it to those in the greatest need. Doing so creates what MacAskill calls "the 100x Multiplier"—his estimate that the resources of those of us in the most economically developed economies can do one hundred times more good for the poorest on earth than we can do for ourselves.[2] On MacAskill's own modest professorial income, he calculates, the amount of benefit the poorest in the world would derive from $1 is about the same as MacAskill would derive from $100.

Throughout this book, we've been revisiting the graph from Chapter 3 that showed how we can create more value for ourselves and for the world. As we have noted, the horizontal axis is far wider than the vertical axis is tall. This is because our ethical behaviors have the potential to do more good for other people than the costs to ourselves. But Stevenson and Wolfers's research, combined with MacAskill's analysis of it, suggests that if this graph were truly accurate, the horizontal axis would be spilling far off the page: it would be about one hundred times as wide as the vertical axis is tall to convey the actual increase in cumulative value of giving up our own outcomes to dramatically affect the outcomes of others. That is, by giving up a very small amount of value, you can create enormous value for others—if you do it effectively.

Transferring our wealth to those most in need is just one of many strategies we can follow to create amazing multipliers. As we'll see, others include rigorously testing new ideas, moving toward System 2 thinking for important decisions, and affecting the decisions of others.

THE MORAL IMPERATIVE TO EXPERIMENT

More than twenty-five years ago, economist Michael Kremer found himself in Kenya, using randomized controlled trials (RCTs) to try to get children to go to school more regularly.[3] He started by testing whether providing textbooks would raise attendance. Some students randomly received the textbooks; others did not. Most of us would probably assume this was a good place to start, but Kremer found that additional textbooks weren't effective at increasing attendance.[4] He then tested the effectiveness of providing flip charts in the classroom. No effect. Then he tried decreasing class size by hiring more teachers. Again, no effect.

Kremer was surprised by how hard it was to get children to go to school, but he kept trying. Next, he decided to try deworming. Intestinal worms are parasitic infections that affect more than one billion people worldwide.[5] These parasites make millions of children sick and can be cured for pennies using readily available drugs. And it turns out that deworming improved school attendance, since infections were keeping kids at home. Not only did deworming work, but the money spent on deworming had a dramatic effect in comparison to other well-intended strategies for getting children to school, with health benefits as a bonus.

What gets children to show up for school is now a well-studied topic, particularly in the field of developmental economics. One recent advance in the social sciences has been the use of comparative analyses that ask "What is the most effective strategy for solving a specific problem?"—such as getting children to go to school. The results show not only that deworming creates an enormous multiple in terms of the effect of an extra $100 donation, but that deworming is far more than one hundred times as effective as many other logical interventions, since many of them have no impact at all.[6] And, while there has been some controversy more recently about the generalizability of the magnitude of the effectiveness of deworming,[7] the logic of using true experiments to assess comparative effectiveness has proliferated in developmental economics and beyond.

Effective altruists and others who simply want to be maximally effective are interested not just in whether an idea works, but also in how it compares to other possible interventions. The logic for getting the best evidence possible on the effectiveness of different interventions is compelling, and something for all of us to consider before we invest scarce funds on a strategy that has less than one one-hundredth of the effect of an alternative strategy. Moving beyond school attendance, amazing evidence exists that we can invest money to improve health and well-being with interventions that are more than one hundred times as effective as other interventions that appear reasonable when considered in isolation.[8]

I mentioned in passing that Kremer used RCTs (also called clinical trials, A/B testing, or simply experiments) to determine that deworming was far more effective at getting children to attend school than lots of other ideas that seemed to make sense prior to testing. Kremer's work, including his innovation of showing the power of RCTs in developmental economics, was key to him receiving the Nobel Prize in economics in 2019. Most of us are familiar with the use of clinical trials in medical contexts. For example, when a pharmaceutical firm has good reason to believe that it has developed a drug that can effectively treat a disease, the U.S. government requires the company to undertake a number of tasks to prevent harmful products from entering the market, including running RCTs to assess the drug's effectiveness. While many people use the word "experiment" to mean "try something new," scientists have a much more specific definition in mind.

Ronald Fisher developed the modern notion of an experiment in 1925.[9] The goal of experiments remains the same today: to find out what works in a scientific manner that allows for causal inference. In recent years, field experiments—rigorous controlled experiments conducted in actual organizations and other real-world settings—have become very popular in developmental economics, the tech sector, and government.[10] Experiments provide a critical tool for finding the biggest multipliers of goodness. The essence of an experiment is to randomly create two or more groups, treat them differently on some variable, and then compare them with respect to a measured response. The experimental group receives the intervention that's being assessed, while the control group has an alternative condition, such as no intervention. Thus, in a pharmaceutical experiment, the treatment group takes the actual medicine, the control group gets a placebo, and neither knows if they are getting the medicine or the placebo. It is only in the new millennium that we have seen true experiments grow to be a common and visible process, across multiple industries, for figuring out what works.[11]

Despite the power of experiments, most organizations test new ideas without a control condition, then subjectively assess whether they were effective, often with a bias toward detecting positive change when little or none actually occurred. Without experiments, the task of making very difficult inferences about whether new ideas worked, as well as the magnitude of the effects, is difficult and error prone. Experiments are the gold standard for finding out what works and how much impact interventions have.

Yet experiments have also come under criticism in recent years. When Facebook ran experiments that manipulated its users' emotions, some were outraged.[12] Some people also view experiments as paternalistic. The libertarian streak that runs through much of the United States recoils at any efforts at manipulation, especially by government entities.[13] I personally have had concerns with how organizations use the results of the experiments they conduct. After cofounding Harvard's Behavioral Insights Group in 2013, I attended meetings with government officials of the many emerging "nudge units" around the globe that were trying to make government work better, often through experimentation (more on nudge units below). At the end of the Obama administration, in December 2016, U.S. census officials arrived on campus seeking advice on how to use experiments to improve the accuracy of the census. I was among the faculty members who chose not to further engage with these well-intended public servants beyond this initial meeting, since they could not guarantee that the incoming Trump administration wouldn't try to use improved census data to identify people eligible for deportation. In 2018, our fears were realized when the Trump administration announced that it intended to ask U.S. residents about their citizenship status on the 2020 census. This action could have led to massive suffering, but was prevented by a variety of court decisions in 2019. At the 2016 meeting with census officials, I noted that the Nazis used demographic census information to round up Jews and other marginalized groups in their genocidal efforts.

More mundane criticisms of experiments fall under the category of "experiment aversion"—people's fear of being "guinea pigs." Many people have an intuitive, System 1 aversion to the idea of being a "subject" in an experiment. More methodical System 2 reasoning generally leads to the views that (1) testing new ideas is good, (2) thinking systematically about what to test and how to test it makes sense, and (3) testing new ideas on a relatively small number of people rather than rolling out an idea that will affect many people without any testing is wise.[14] Together, these logical thought processes suggest that running experiments provides overall benefits.

Experimentation is simply a method for trying new ideas in a systematic manner. It's also an active component of the effective altruism movement. Noting the problems caused by relying on charities' self-serving and biased data, GiveWell concludes that academic experiments often provide better answers. Academics have less motivation than organizational leaders to produce biased results, and the academic peer review process helps to ensure high-quality evidence. The precision of the experimental method also adds protection. But not all are convinced. Peter Singer quotes Elizabeth Bintliff, the vice president of Heifer International's Africa programs, whose organization does not do well by effective altruism standards, as saying, "We're not about experiments. These are lives of real people, and we have to believe that what we believe is correct. We can't make experiments with people's lives. They're just . . . they're people. It's too important."[15] Of course, it's because people's lives matter that we need the best available evidence, which experiments can help to provide. Stated more forcefully, if we want to do as much good as we can, we have a moral imperative to experiment. Just like arithmetic and analytic skills, experiments in the wrong hands can create harm. But for those of us who want to do more good, experiments are a useful tool. Overall, the effective altruism movement, and MacAskill's writing in particular, have done a great job of highlighting how philanthropy can have a dramatic multiplier on the effectiveness of your donations when it's driven by deliberative thinking and evidence.

MULTIPLYING BY NUDGING OTHERS

Many of us—including parents, business leaders, and public officials—are responsible not only for our own decisions, but for the decisions of others. We can influence others' decisions by creating motivational systems, providing guidance, and altering the environment in which decisions will be made. The latter is often called choice architecture, or nudging, a concept that Richard Thaler and Cass Sunstein introduced in their 2008 book, *Nudge*. Drawing on the work of psychologists such as Kahneman, Tversky, Cialdini, and others, *Nudge* highlighted that while we know little about how to debias our cognitive imperfections, we understand human cognition well enough that we can redesign the "architecture" surrounding our choices so that people will make wiser decisions as a result.

A classic example of nudging is to encourage the desired behavior by changing the default choice that decision makers face. Default options are predetermined courses of action that take effect if the decision maker does not proactively take any action. The simple idea is that we make many decisions in life passively simply by accepting the default. We sign standard contracts. We use the web browser that's preinstalled on our computer. Many people also accept the default retirement program offered by their employer, rather than thinking through what makes the most sense for them.

The fact that defaults sway our decisions—and our lives—seems obvious, but defaults end up mattering far more than our intuition suggests. A classic example of the power of defaults comes from the world of organ donations. In many states, U.S. citizens can choose to agree to donate their organs when applying for a driver's license or another ID. In these states, you aren't in the organ donation system unless you actively choose to be—that's the default. What would happen if your state automatically enrolled you in the organ donation system unless you opted out? Studying organ donation policies and rates in eleven European countries, psychologists Eric Johnson and Dan Goldstein found that the four countries with opt-in systems had organ donation rates between 4 and 28 percent, while the seven with opt-out systems had donation rates ranging from 86 to 100 percent.[16] If our primary goal is to save the most lives possible, opt-out policies are clearly superior to opt-in choice. Yet many U.S. states maintain the ineffective strategy of requiring citizens to opt in, and thousands of Americans die each year due to the shortage of organs.[17]

In *Nudge*, Thaler and Sunstein document many other enormously effective nudges: making healthy options more accessible in cafeterias, increasing voting rates by encouraging people to plan their voting-day activities in advance, and providing text reminders to be vaccinated against predictable and preventable diseases. Based on the ideas in *Nudge*, the program Save More Tomorrow encourages workers to commit to increasing their retirement savings rates in advance of a pay increase and to continue to do so with each raise until they reach a preset maximum.[18] Employees can opt out of the program at any time, but most don't, and the results have been dramatic increases in savings rates.

Not only does nudging allow you to influence a large number of people to be better, but it is a very cost-effective strategy. Shlomo Benartzi, John Beshears, Katy Milkman, and their colleagues compared the cost-effectiveness of nudging for increasing retirement savings, increasing college enrollment, improving energy conservation, and getting people to be vaccinated against a number of the most effective alternative strategies.[19] (See the figure on the next page for details.) The evidence clearly supports the power of nudging to be an amazing multiplier in our ability to do good.

So-called nudge units are using choice architecture to create value around the globe. The Behavioural Insights Team (BIT) in the United Kingdom—the first of its kind—has drawn on findings from behavioral science research to implement numerous policy

Retirement Savings (Increase in Contributions for the Year per $1 Spent)

Active-Decision Nudge (Carroll et al., 2009)	$100
Danish Tax Incentives (Chetty et al., 2014)	$2.77
Retirement Savings Information (Duflo & Saez, 2003)	$14.58
Matching Contributions: 20% (Duflo et al., 2006)	$5.59
Matching Contributions: 50% (Duflo et al., 2006)	$2.97
U.S. Tax Incentives (Duflo et al., 2007)	$1.24

College Enrollment (Increase in Students Enrolled per $1,000 Spent)

Form-Streamlining Nudge (Bettinger et al., 2012)	1.53
Monthly Stipends (Dynarski, 2003)	0.0351
Monetary Subsidies (Long, 2004a)	0.0051
Tax Credits (Long, 2004b; Bulman & Hoxby, 2015)	Negligible

Energy Conservation (Increase in kWh Saved per $1 Spent)

Social-Norms Nudge (Allcott, 2011)	27.3
Health-Linked Usage Information Nudge (Asensio & Delmas, 2015)	0.050
Billing-Information Nudge (Asensio & Delmas, 2015)	Negligible
Electricity Bill Discounts (Ito, 2015)	3.41
Incentives and Education (Arimura et al., 2012)	14.0

Influenza Vaccinations (Increase in Adults Vaccinated per $100 Spent)

Planning-Prompt Nudge (Milkman et al., 2011)	12.8
Default-Appointment Nudge (Chapman et al., 2010)	3.65
Monetary Incentive (Bronchetti et al., 2015)	1.78
Educational Campaign (Kimura et al., 2007)	8.85
Free Work-Site Vaccinations (Kimura et al., 2007)	1.07

■ Nudge   ☐ Traditional Intervention (financial incentives, educational programs, or some combination of the two) changes, to great economic and popular success. BIT has completed about one thousand field experiments, all aimed at using psychological thought and field experimentation to demonstrate better ways to run the government. They have improved school attendance, diversified recruitment in police forces, reduced no-shows to medical appointments, and more.

Virtually anyone in a leadership role can use choice architecture as a tool to guide others to make wise decisions that create value for themselves and society. In many cases, making fairly minor changes to forms can improve hundreds, even thousands, of decisions. By doing so, we multiply our ability to create good in the world.

CREATING NETWORKS OF GIVERS

Marla, my spouse, has had many careers (corporate, academic, consultant, expert witness, education and consumer advocate, investigative journalist, political blogger, and philanthropist). Marla is only partially persuaded by the effective altruism movement. She has spent time with academic and professional leaders in the effective altruism world, but her charitable preferences aren't in agreement with theirs. However, Marla is a multiplier. Many people are influenced by her views. People go out of their way to get her opinions. Our living room is often filled with people being influenced by Marla's passions.

One of Marla's obsessions is the fact that we know many people who do just fine in life, but, from her perspective, give too little to people in need. Here Marla is aligned with MacAskill. When people end up in our living room, Marla does an amazing job of convincing them to give some of their excess wealth to whatever charity she's championing that day. One would think that this would make visiting our house less attractive, but Marla is also warm, witty, and fun to talk to—qualities that doubtless contribute to her ability to bring many hundreds of people through our home every year.

More formally, as mentioned earlier, Marla is the cofounder of The Philanthropy Connection (TPC), an organization whose mission is to inspire women to pool their funding to provide grants to charitable organizations that serve low-resource individuals and families living in Massachusetts. Marla created TPC with the notion that people (specifically, women) would contribute more if they knew more about the needs of people in their area and could easily meet and develop personal connections with nonprofit leaders.

TPC focuses on the argument that many women are willing and able to give more, but don't, simply because they have not been asked or because they don't have enough information to be confident that their donation will be put to good use. (Marla would say the same about men, but chose to focus her organization on women.) Women pay $1,175 per year to be a member of TPC. Of that amount, $1,000 is committed to organizations that receive funding through a democratic process. The remaining $175 per year is used for expenses and the social events that bring the community (TPC members and the organizations that they fund) together. TPC members often go on to multiply their impact by donating their time to the nonprofit organizations they have been introduced to through TPC, serving on their boards, and making larger donations.

Consider the impact that TPC had on Silver Lining Mentoring (SLM), a nonprofit organization that empowers youth in foster care to thrive through committed mentoring relationships and the development of essential life skills. TPC awarded SLM $56,000 across two different yearly funding cycles. Beyond this direct support, the exposure that SLM received from TPC generated another thirty individual donors and more than $270,000 in additional funding, according to Colby Swettberg, the dynamic former executive director of SLM (and now the chief executive officer of its sister organization, the Silver Lining Institute). SLM hired a TPC member as its development director. And SLM also met Dr. Anna Vouros thanks to TPC.

Dr. Vouros, a primary care physician at Massachusetts General Hospital, was interested in better connecting to the nonprofit community in Boston, but her busy schedule created a barrier to finding the right connection. She joined TPC, and through TPC learned about SLM, an organization that inspired her philanthropic interests. Dr. Vouros soon joined the SLM board, became a leader within the board, served on the SLM governance committee, introduced SLM to her peer network, hosted events for SLM, recruited her colleagues and friends for SLM fundraising events, and purchased items at SLM fundraising auctions (like throwing out at the first pitch at Fenway Park). In addition to doing good for others, Dr. Vouros finds this activity fulfilling.

TPC members also report that they start giving away more of their money to organizations that aren't funded by TPC because of connections made through TPC. TPC's direct and spillover effects clearly create much good. Yet, from an effective altruist's perspective, the funding that TPC distributes isn't doing as much good as it could. After all, TPC only funds organizations in the Boston metropolitan area; by contrast, as we learned in Chapter 9, the effective altruism world argues that we can multiply our impact by sending our funds overseas, where donations are more cost-effective. But Marla and TPC are multipliers nonetheless—maybe not because of the specific causes they fund, but because of the transformation they inspire in givers.

Effective altruism encourages donors to focus on engaging in cognitive deliberation to identify how their funds can do the most good. Marla and TPC encourage clear and rigorous assessments of the operations of the charities they consider funding, but they also foster emotional connections that prompt members to give and keep giving. Notably, without those emotional connections, the givers likely would not be spending their money on malaria prevention in Africa, but rather would leave more money to their children. By providing knowledge and social connections, Marla has the unique ability to unleash people's hidden philanthropic desires.

As someone who's more convinced by the effective altruism movement, it obviously occurs to me that TPC could have focused on raising money for the most effective causes. But Marla, correctly, would respond that most TPC members would not connect to an organization that spent most of its donations to help people thousands of miles from the United States or to save chickens from suffering. Marla multiplies the number of givers rather than QALYs created by each donated dollar.

TEACHING YOUR VALUES

As I've mentioned, I teach negotiation—a lot! I have been teaching negotiation to MBA and executive students since 1984. I have taught negotiation at the Sloan School at MIT, the Kellogg School at Northwestern, the Harvard Kennedy School of Government, and the Harvard Business School. I have also taught in corporate programs for dozens of well-known corporations in thirty countries. A quick estimate is that I have taught more than thirty thousand people, in person, how to negotiate more effectively. Fortunately, I like to teach negotiation.

When people hear that I teach negotiation, they imagine that

I teach people how to get a good price and/or to get people to do what you want them to do. It's true that I do some of this. But I do much more of something that's broader and more important: I teach my students to think about the decisions of others, to understand others' needs, and to find opportunities to create value. Negotiation scholars view most complex negotiations as consisting of a tension between the need to create value and the need to claim it, as I briefly described in Chapter 3.[20] One of the most important ways in which a negotiation teacher can create value in the world is to help hundreds or thousands of students create value themselves by busting their mythical fixed-pie mindset and identifying creative, mutually beneficial solutions.

Negotiators are often nervous about sharing information about their interests, for fear the other party will use that information to claim value. But sharing information is an important part of creating value with your counterpart. As a teacher, I can influence students to appreciate the long-term benefits of value creation more than the short-term concern of losing on the value-claiming side. In the process, we move toward the North Star of maximizing positive benefit for all.

Beyond negotiation, like other teachers, I get to make lots of decisions about what and how I teach, decisions that could have a long-term impact on many of my students. I get to decide how much to focus on the ethical dimensions of the topics I teach. Though I'm teaching, not preaching, I get to decide when to share my views about what constitutes a moral decision in a given situation. I can decide to discuss politics when doing so could influence my students to create more value. Most teachers have such choices, and I encourage all teachers to think about the value they can create.

We teachers also get to influence the norms of others by how we lead our lives. Do we find time to talk to the student who needs advice on a problem that is bothering them? Do we spend five minutes on an email that will significantly benefit someone else, perhaps someone we will never meet? As Dolly Chugh asks, do we take the thirty seconds needed to learn a student's name so that they will feel more respected and seen?[21] Not only can we create value by the way we lead our lives, but as teachers, we can create norms that others may follow.

In addition to teaching tens of thousands of students, I have also been very involved in training the next generation of scholars in negotiation, behavioral economics, and ethics. I have spent many thousands of hours focused on collaborating and mentoring a couple dozen amazing scholars in the generation that will follow me. I'm proud of the figure on my website, https://scholar.harvard.edu/bazerman/advisee-network, which depicts not only my students, but my students' students, and so on (the vast majority of whom are now professors). And I'm proud of the fact that my broad research group is a community, one that knows it is in the business of value creation. These successful professors are thriving in a way that creates value in the world. Todd Rogers (professor, Harvard Kennedy School) may have done more to get adults to vote and children to show up at school than any human on the planet. Don Moore (professor, Berkeley's Haas School of Business, author of *Perfectly Confident,* and coauthor of *Judgment in Managerial Decision Making*) is a critical scholar in improving how we make decisions. Ann Tenbrunsel (professor, Notre Dame, coauthor of *Blind Spots*) is one of the foremost scholars in behavioral ethics. Dolly Chugh's (professor, New York University, author of *The Person You Mean to Be*) TED talk has challenged more than four million people to live up to their ethical standards (and has obviously influenced the "better" theme of this book). And Katy Milkman (professor, Penn's Wharton School, author of *Change for Good*) has focused her enormous talents on how to scale behavioral change that makes the world better. Sorry to brag, but there are a bunch of other mentees of mine who have done other amazing things. Our community of scholars has a clear norm to help others, particularly when a small amount of effort by one person can create large value for another.

These scholars strangely give me some of the credit for their success, nominate me for nice awards, and act as if I sacrificed for them. The not-too-secret secret is that no sacrifice was involved in mentoring them. By working with them, my life became better. That's in large part why I spent so much time mentoring: The more I did, the more I received, and the world was better as a result. This is the nature of successful collaboration, mentoring, and teaching. And it's consistent with Liz Dunn and Michael Norton's research showing that giving away money (or, I would argue, time, though they didn't test this) is a very successful strategy for increasing your own happiness.[22]

By the way, all of us are teachers, not just those of us who get paid for the task. Parents are teachers. Coaches and mentors are teachers. So are politicians and managers. When we teach well, we can influence how our students create value for decades to come.

TAKING RISKS

In 1798, the English cleric and scholar Thomas Malthus argued that the human population was growing far faster than our ability to create enough food to feed everyone and that without interventions, the world was headed toward massive disease epidemics, premature death, starvation, and war, or what his followers referred to as a "Malthusian catastrophe." But while many terrible events have occurred in the two-hundred-plus years since

Malthus's prediction, and the human population has grown significantly, no Malthusian catastrophe happened. Malthus underestimated the human capacity to innovate, and that entrepreneurial capacity is at least part of the reason why society has thrived.[23]

American agronomist Norman Borlaug isn't a household name, but some credit him for avoiding a Malthusian crisis and saving as many as a billion lives. Malthus assumed that we would continue to increase our food production linearly. But during the Green Revolution, a period of agricultural development between the 1940s and the late 1970s, many efficient new agricultural innovations took place, including high-yielding varieties of cereal grains, the modernization of management techniques, and the distribution of hybridized seeds and synthetic fertilizers to farmers. Borlaug developed a high-yield, parasite-resistant wheat hybrid that grew in numerous climates, regardless of the amount of daytime light. Borlaug's "dwarf variety" solved the problem of tall wheat expending a great deal of energy growing inedible stalks and collapsing when they grew too quickly.

Borlaug's work started in North America, but by the 1960s, he focused his attention on India and Pakistan, and was central to ending the famines that were common across Southeast Asia. His work increased wheat harvests by 600 percent in India and Pakistan from the early 1960s to the late 1970s; for the first time, the subcontinent became a net wheat exporter. Borlaug went on to win the Nobel Peace Prize, the Congressional Gold Medal, and the Presidential Medal of Freedom.

Many experts predict that we will be unable to produce enough protein for the world's population by 2050. But these predictions are based on current methods for producing animal protein and ignore the revolution that is happening in the Good Food Movement. Specifically, they ignore the possibility that we will soon be able to produce actual animal protein in a much more sustainable manner, without harming additional animals. We don't know whether Uma Valeti and Memphis Meats, whom you met in Chapter 8, will be key to solving this predicted protein shortage, but it is clear that those who innovate to solve such problems have enormous potential to create value, beyond the products that they themselves create. Notably, however, scientists and entrepreneurs who try to innovate to create enormous value take on risky bets and must be willing to risk failure. This willingness to accept uncertainty is part of the process of creating multipliers for the future.

Few people can multiply their impact to the degree that Norman Borlaug did, but all of us can do far better by thinking about how we can create more value. Whether we are more generous, are more thoughtful about our generosity, influence others, or innovate, striving to multiply our value creation can allow us to be far better.

CHAPTER 11

MAXIMUM SUSTAINABLE GOODNESS

In the spring of 2019, when I had about half of the chapters of this book drafted, I attended a talk given by Mark Budolfson, a philosopher at the University of Vermont who was visiting the Safra Center for Ethics at Harvard for the academic year. Mark spoke at Safra about how to compare the pain and pleasure of different animal species, a topic that I found fascinating. I emailed him afterward and asked him to get together to discuss his talk. When we met, I described my ideas about the goal of being better, not perfect. He followed up on that meeting with an email, in which he suggested that the overview I'd given him of the book you're now reading "connects to the concept of sustainability, as it focuses on finding the 'maximum sustainable level' of altruism." He continued, "In this way, it is similar to the idea of managing a mature fishery by aiming for the maximum sustainable (economic) yield." I tweaked Mark's comment to come up with the concept of "maximum sustainable goodness."

Mark was referring to the environmental management concept of "maximum sustainable yield" (MSY). The concept of MSY aims to maintain the population size at the point of maximum growth rate by harvesting the individuals that would normally be added to the population, allowing the population to continue to be productive indefinitely. MSY is different from the maximum catch or harvest possible in the current year, since if you catch all of the fish in a fishing basin, there won't be any fish left to create more fish for you in the future. It turns out that lots of people have thought about MSY, starting with fisheries in Belmar, New Jersey, in the 1930s.[1] MSY is a commonly used concept in the environmental world to describe environmentally appropriate behavior.[2]

I've argued in this book that if we push for far more than our maximum sustainable goodness—say, for pure utilitarianism or perfect justice—we may reject the goal as unreasonable or unobtainable; not to mention, our efforts could discourage others from even trying to do better. By comparison, the goal of being better, while not perfect, is more viable. We can try to think about how much value we can create so that we can continue to lead a purposeful and enjoyable life, with the hope of further increasing our capacity to create even more goodness in the future. For most of us, this will translate into a moderate increase in our value creation this year in comparison to last year. I've found that people tend to find this goal reasonable, motivating, and helpful.

This idea also nicely maps onto the latest United Nations report on climate change, which warns that unless humans change their diet, efforts to curb greenhouse gas emissions will fall short of even pessimistic earlier predictions. Focusing on the land used to raise cattle and other meat-producing livestock, this Intergovernmental Panel on Climate Change report calls on people in wealthy nations to reduce meat consumption and move toward plant-based diets. Why not just encourage people to become vegetarians? "We don't want to tell people what to eat," said Hans-Otto Pörtner, a member of the report committee.[3] The committee likely realized that many well-intentioned meat eaters would ignore a recommendation to become vegetarians but be open to seriously considering reducing their level of meat consumption.

CAN I KEEP THIS UP?

At the effective altruism conference in 2018 that I mentioned at the start of Chapter 1, I was interviewed in front of the large audience of people who endorsed effective altruism. The first question the interviewer asked me was "Do you consider yourself an effective altruist?"[4] I had a complex reaction to this question, but since the interviewer asked for a yes or no, I started with "no." I then mentioned that, because I was speaking in front of a couple hundred people who identified as effective altruists, I didn't want to claim a status that I frequently undermined with imperfect behaviors, such as eating dairy, wearing leather, not donating 50 percent of my income to charity, and donating to causes that would not be selected by the effective altruism community. I argued that for all of us, the effectiveness of our altruism, and our moral behavior more broadly, can be found on an ever-changing continuum. But the question I was asked is relevant to my reasons for writing this book. I've attempted to describe what perfection looks like, what barriers keep us from reaching this state, and how we can move in the right direction. As a result of this exploration, I think I'm creating more value this year than I did when I was asked that question in 2018. So, I would assess myself now as a more effective altruist!

In his book *10% Happier*, ABC correspondent Dan Harris argues that mindfulness won't solve all of our problems, but, when implemented effectively, it can make us 10 percent happier.[5] I am agnostic on mindfulness, but I appreciate Harris's acknowledgment that it is not reasonable to expect any particular self-help intervention to make us completely happy, but that 10 percent happier would be a great and realistic accomplishment. Similarly, if you can create 10 percent more value in the world in the year ahead than you created in the past year, that would be an excellent accomplishment. While hard to measure, 10 percent sounds like a difficult yet achievable goal. By comparison, to most of us, 70 percent or 80 percent more value sounds unreasonable. (But if you think you can meet it, go for it!) All of us can consider maximally sustainable changes we can make in our goodness, from those that simply require engaging our active intelligence to those that might require some sacrifices to make the world better, even if it won't make us perfect.

Another parallel for thinking about maximally sustainable goodness might be our diets. I am tall (6'2") and not visibly overweight, but about fifteen years ago, I discovered that my lipid levels were terrible, particularly my triglycerides. After some research, I found Dr. Frank Sacks, a Boston cardiologist who has done foundational research on lipids. The recipe he ordered for me was to take a statin, exercise more, and reduce the unhealthy fats in my diet. By then, I was already a vegetarian, and my diet was fairly healthy. Thus, having bad lipids that were a threat to my health was a bit frustrating. I really like interesting food and consuming a moderate level of alcohol. So, how could I balance these pleasures with my desire for a long and healthy life? First, I stopped paying for a Harvard parking pass, which forced me to walk to work, nudging me toward ten thousand steps a day.

Second, spurred by Dr. Sacks, I made a series of wise food trades. I was happy to give up butter for olive oil. I stopped eating mediocre bread, but still eat great bread when it is in front of me. I cut back dramatically on ice cream. I still eat great pizza, which I love, but avoid mediocre pizza. Regarding alcohol, I like cabernets (particularly Silver Oak, Sequoia Grove, Groth, and Stonestreet, in case you were wondering) and stouts (such as Sam Smith's Chocolate Stout). When I did some research, I found out that cabernet was much healthier for me than stouts, so my cabernet drinking increased at the expense of the stout makers. No more cookies or pie, and fewer chips. While the changes took some adjustment, they required little suffering. Overall, my diet got better, my lipid levels improved dramatically, and I still get to eat great meals. I think I found a maximally sustainable diet!

Peter Singer highlights that doing the most good we can, from a practical standpoint, requires us to be a well-adjusted human being.[6] He describes the struggle that Julia Wise, a visible effective altruist in the Boston area, faced when deciding whether to have children. As an effective altruist, she was concerned that the costs of raising children (food, education, college, etc.) would take away from her and her spouse's ability to donate as much as possible to charity. But she also understood that not having children would create enough emotional downside and unhappiness that it would make her less effective in many other ways at making the world better. As I write this in 2019, Julia is the president of Giving What We Can, serves on the board of GiveWell, and writes about effective altruism at "Giving Gladly." She and her husband are also the proud parents of a five-year-old and a three-year-old, and they continue to donate half of their income to the most effective charities they can find. Julia seems to have figured out how to be far better without trying to be perfect.

INFLUENCING OTHERS—IN A SUSTAINABLE MANNER

Imagine that you have a goal of reducing the consumption of animals as much as possible. You are open to nudging your friends toward reducing their animal consumption as well. You are meeting a friend for lunch, and after you get to the restaurant, which you have been to multiple times, he texts you to say that he's running a little late, and asks you to order him a veggie burger. He is a carnivore and hasn't been to the restaurant before, and you realize he might be trying to be polite, given your diet. You immediately see this as an opportunity to move him toward eating more plant-based products. The two options on the menu, both of which you have had before, are a great-tasting vegetarian burger (not vegan; they use some egg to moisten the burger and bind ingredients) and a dry, bland vegan burger that you didn't like at all. Which do you order for your carnivore friend? In his book *How to Create a Vegan World: A Pragmatic Approach*, Tobias Leenaert argues that while the vegan burger might be the more idealistic choice, the vegetarian burger is more likely to have a positive impact on your friend—and to create maximum sustainable goodness.[7] Thus, to move others toward greater goodness, it is useful to think about what level of change is viable and sustainable. More broadly, the best way to influence others is to think about their mindset, rather than focusing on an unobtainable ideal state—something that I failed to do in the opening anecdote of this book when I teased a stranger about being a "fisheterian."

IS IT OKAY TO ENJOY YOUR INCREASED GOODNESS?

The French philosopher Auguste Comte, who coined the term "altruism," defined it as "self-sacrifice for the benefit of others," where "the only moral acts were those intended to promote the happiness of others."[8] According to Comte, if an action was performed for reasons beyond improving the well-being of others, it was not morally justified. If you get a tax deduction for a charitable donation, that donation is no longer altruistic, according to Comte's extreme view. If you enjoy your act of generosity or see it as "enlightened self-interest," it also fails Comte's standard for altruism. Once again, I find the standards of a philosopher to be too extreme. No one can meet Comte's standard, and this realization is likely to lead people to not try and to limit the value that they actually create. I prefer the following viewpoint expressed by Martin Luther King Jr., "Every man must decide whether he will walk in the light of creative altruism or in the darkness of destructive selfishness."[9] King clearly believed that being creatively altruistic would lead to a more meaningful and enjoyable life.

Evolutionary scholars believe that altruism has evolutionary roots—that cooperation and generosity promote the survival of the species. But there are other, more System 2–like bases for altruism. Altruism is one aspect of what social psychologists refer to as prosocial behavior—actions that benefit other people, no matter what the motive or how the giver benefits. Psychologists have suggested many reasons we engage in prosocial behavior: doing so activates pleasure centers in the brain, allows us to experience positive reinforcement for being nice, enables us to meet social norms, and has emotional benefits. Because these benefits accrue to the altruist, they're all inconsistent with Comte's definition of altruism. Some psychologists believe that true Comteian altruism exists; others think that it does not—that we always get something out of the deal. I have often heard people criticize altruistic acts as having some secondary motive, such as "They do it for the recognition." Yet, virtually all (if not all) behaviors that

we might define as altruistic—behaviors we want to encourage—
have some potential to benefit the altruist, in Comte's view. We
should embrace the benefits that people get from their altruism,
rather than criticizing them, as they are on the path of creating
more value.

There are exceptions to this conclusion. For example, I don't endorse charitable contributions connected to corruption, like in the
academic legacy story detailed earlier. Thus, if someone "buys"
their way into an elite institution, I don't endorse this action, as
this corruption reduces value for reasons we covered in Chapter 4. But if people take pride in creating value, or even want to
be publicly acknowledged for doing so, we should give them that
credit—which will encourage more value creation in the process.
There's nothing wrong with being proud of doing better, and that
pride doesn't take away from the intrinsic merits of our acts. In
fact, adding extrinsic reasons to the intrinsic reasons for creating
value adds up to a formula for doing far better.

Some people fear that following a utilitarian North Star takes
the fun out of being better. We all know people who have tremen-
dous passion for a cause—often, a cause that effective altruism
would not recommend. Does trying to maximize our goodness
come at the cost of a loss of passion? Does it require too much cognition and not enough emotion? Both of these are reasonable concerns. Yet I see amazing passion in the ideas and actions of people
like Uma Valeti and Bruce Friedrich as they try to figure out how
to do the most good possible. Even without knowing which people
or animals they are helping, or without meeting those that benefit
from their behaviors, they take enormous pride in the very high
level of sustainable goodness they are able to create. Personally, I
aspire to create more good, while also enjoying my role in creating
greater goodness.

THE PATH FORWARD

Perhaps you are the kind of person who likes to assess how you are doing. So, have you reached your maximum sustainable goodness? The good news is that we have some acceptable metrics for this question: How does the total of your charitable contributions this year compare to last year? How effective are the organizations that you contributed to this year in comparison to last year? Are you being more thoughtful about your moral choices? Are you avoiding waste and using your time more wisely? Are you actively aiming to treat people and other creatures with whom we share the earth with greater equality? Are you thinking about future generations and doing more to protect them?

Answering these questions is probably a much more pleasant task than thinking about whether you are reaching a philosophical definition of morality. But you probably want to go beyond reviewing the past and start thinking about the future. So, if you are with me on the idea of being better next year than last, how do you get there? For me, part of the answer is to start with some easy wins. As you consider how you make decisions, think about how you provide help to others, how you make trade-offs, what you waste, and how you make charitable decisions. Are your current actions what you would recommend to others? If not, why not—and how can you kick your old habits and create new ones? Over the last ten years, I have thought more carefully about when I say yes, given more to charity than in the past, made wiser decisions about who gets our charitable dollars, tried to be helpful to my intellectual community, offered my time to important philanthropic groups, and tried to be more environmentally conscientious.

Yet I remain very far from the North Star of utilitarian behavior. Next year I will get closer, while still remaining far away, on this fascinating pathway toward my maximum sustainable level of goodness. I hope that this book helps you along a similar path.

ACKNOWLEDGMENTS

I entered the University of Pennsylvania as an accounting major with the intention of looking for a real-world job after completing my undergraduate degree. A practical eighteen-year-old, I never considered taking a philosophy course. I only wish I'd known then how practical philosophy could be.

Much later, in 1990–91, I was involved in a search for a new chaired professorship in ethics at the Kellogg Graduate School of Management at Northwestern, a daunting task at the time. Back then, there was no field of behavioral ethics in business schools, and finding a scholar with academic credentials who was qualified to receive tenure at Northwestern was tough. I was central to proposing that we recruit David Messick, a psychology professor at the University of California, Santa Barbara. David was a well-respected social psychologist who studied fairness, social comparison processes, and a host of other interpersonal processes relevant to ethics. My goal was to help the school solve a complicated recruiting challenge; the idea that this hiring decision would change my research trajectory wasn't even a distant thought.

Around the time David came to Kellogg, Ann Tenbrunsel entered our doctoral program, and she worked both with David and with me. Gradually, we all worked together. But I clearly thought of David and Ann as the ethics people in Kellogg's Organization Behavior department. I identified as a decision-making and negotiation researcher and teacher. Yet by the time I left Kellogg for Harvard at the end of the last millennium, a reasonable chunk of my research was connected to ethical issues.

This budding interest in behavioral ethics was invigorated at Harvard, as I spent time and wrote papers with Dolly Chugh and Mahzarin Banaji, and learned more about the psychology of ethical behavior. Our work developed the notion of bounded ethicality, or the predictable and systematic ways in which even good people engage in bad behaviors.

In 2005, Joshua Greene joined the psychology department at Harvard. He and I quickly connected over lunch in March 2006, finding that we agreed on many ethical issues. Josh, who is squarely in the camp of utilitarian philosophers, received his doctorate from Princeton in philosophy and then did his postdoc in neuro-social psychology. Since 2006, Josh and I have coauthored a number of papers; far more important for me, Josh has been my personal tutor in philosophy. When I met Josh, I knew very little about philosophy. As we worked together, I was consistently struck by Josh's clarity of thought and by the North Star that he brought to most ethical analyses. Much of what you read in this book is rooted in conversations with Josh.

This book has taken a long time to write, often due to my need to step back and read more philosophy. The more I read, the better sense I had of what I was trying to achieve. Over and over again, I found great clarity in the writings of Peter Singer (for example, *Practical Ethics*). When I talked to Josh about his own amazing book, *Moral Tribes*, he would often note that Singer had written about a related topic long ago. As I developed this book, I similarly felt that I was being heavily influenced by the prior writings of both Greene and Singer. I hope that I have been able to provide some new insights to their works.

I also benefited greatly by wandering into the Good Food Movement, which is made up of people who are motivated to reduce animal suffering by creating new plant-based proteins and cultivated meats that will meet the worldwide demand for protein without the animal suffering involved in our current system. As you have seen, this world of alternative protein has influenced me greatly since 2018. My guides in this journey include Rachel Atcheson, Amy Trakinski, Bruce Friedrich, Aylon Steinhart, Sebastiano Cossia Castiglioni, Mark Langley, Susan Vitka, Lisa Feria, Nina Gheihman, Macy Marriott, and David Welch. Many of these fascinating vegans don't even share the core philosophical perspective in this book, yet they have helped me think through my own ideas with much greater clarity.

Many of my friends know that I have been obsessed about this book for a very long time. I have talked about these ideas and tested them in academic presentations. More recently, I shared early drafts of chapters of the whole book with a number of friends and colleagues. Quite simply, the amount of insightful comments that I have received is stunning, and this book is far better as a result.

Philosophers Josh Greene, Peter Singer, Will MacAskill, Lucius Caviola, and Mark Budolfson read an earlier draft of the book and generously kept me straight on what different philosophical perspectives actually say. Ann Tenbrunsel (my coauthor of *Blind Spots*) and Dolly Chugh read the book in detail, provided amazing feedback, and kept my representation of the empirical literature on behavioral ethics accurate. Katy Milkman provided wonderful clarity on how to express my ideas to have greater impact.

Marla Felcher (my spouse) and Margo Beth Fleming (my agent) read lots of drafts of stuff that is no longer here, profoundly reshaping the structure of the book. I sent psychologist Doug Medin the book to confirm the opening story, and he sent me thoughtful comments covering the entire book. I recently met Dr. Kathryn Reed, a gynecologist at the University of Arizona, when she was taking executive programs at the Harvard Business School. Kathryn quickly became an insightful reviewer of much of my recent work, including this book. Linda Babcock and Laurie Weingart, central characters in Chapter 8, provided clarity on a number of conceptual issues. Mario Small was the most critical of all of my readers, bringing a useful sociological perspective to question my interpretation of numerous issues. I've changed many arguments due to Mario's input. Justin Wolfers generously provided input on Chapter 10. My former colleague Abby Dalton, now at the World Bank, provided her insightful clarity throughout.

Additional helpful comments came from surprising sources. The guy who built the house that Marla, Becca (dog), and I live in in Cambridge, Massachusetts, Martin Cafasso, just happens to have a graduate degree in philosophy from Oxford. In addition to being a fine designer and home builder, he also found time to read this book and provide me with unique insight throughout. My distant cousin Stu Baserman found me due to my prior writing on ethics, hired me as a consultant to reduce dishonesty in the insurance business, became a good friend, and offered a bunch of wisdom on earlier drafts of chapters that I hope are now far better. And Mark Langley and Rachel Atcheson, both core activists in the Good Food Movement, provided insight well beyond the alternative food movement, improving the book substantially in the process.

My faculty support specialist at Harvard, Elizabeth Sweeny, provided excellent editorial support throughout this process. Both

Stephanie Hitchcock and Hollis Heimbouch served as editors of this project for Harper Business and provided important editorial direction. And, as is true for all of my books, Katie Shonk, my personal editor, improved the ideas and the vast majority of sentences throughout the book. I often get compliments on my writing, which I do my best to redirect to where they belong—Katie.

As I reflect on this book, I am stunned to see how many people have helped to improve it. I also realize how different and how much better the book is as a result of their input. I have never written a book that has required such a thorough learning process from me. I thank all of these generous people for the gift of their time, their writing skills, and their ideas. All of them have made this book better, and as you have read, better is what I strive to be.

NOTES

CHAPTER 1: BETTER, NOT PERFECT

1. Behavioral Insights Interview with Max Bazerman—EAGxBoston 2018, April 21, 2018. https://www.youtube.com/watch?v=B8TOz25ctGw.
2. Max H. Bazerman and Ann E. Tenbrunsel, *Blind Spots: Why We Fail to Do What's Right and What to Do about It* (Princeton, NJ: Princeton University Press, 2011).
3. Ibid.
4. Howard Raiffa, *The Art and Science of Negotiation* (Cambridge, MA: Belknap Press of Harvard University Press, 1982).
5. Margaret A. Neale and Max H. Bazerman, *Cognition and Rationality in Negotiation* (New York: Free Press, 1991); Margaret A. Neale and Max H. Bazerman, "Negotiator Cognition and Rationality: A Behavioral Decision Theory Perspective," *Organizational Behavior & Human Decision Processes* 51, no. 2 (1992): 157–75.
6. Baruch Fischhoff, "Debiasing," in *Judgment under Uncertainty: Heuristics and Biases*, ed. Daniel Kahneman, Paul Slovic, and Amos Tversky (Cambridge, MA: Cambridge University Press, 1982), 422–32; Max H. Bazerman and Don Moore, *Judgment in Managerial Decision Making*, 8th ed. (Hoboken, NJ: John Wiley, 2013).
7. Don A. Moore, *Perfectly Confident: How to Calibrate Your Decisions Wisely* (New York: Harper Business, 2020).
8. Keith E. Stanovich and Richard F. West, "Individual Differences in Reasoning: Implications for the Rationality Debate," *Behavioral & Brain Sciences* 23 (2000): 645–65; Daniel Kahneman, "A Perspective on Judgment and Choice: Mapping Bounded Rationality," *American Psychologist* 58 (2003): 697–720.
9. Daniel Kahneman, *Thinking, Fast and Slow* (New York: Farrar, Straus & Giroux, 2011).
10. Richard H. Thaler and Cass Sunstein, *Nudge: Improving Decisions About Health, Wealth, and Happiness* (New Haven, CT: Yale University Press, 2008).

11.   Adapted from Philippa Foot, *Virtues and Vices* (Oxford: Blackwell, 1978); Judith
        Jarvis Thomson, "Killing, Letting Die, and the Trolley Problem," *The Monist 59*,
        no. 2 (2011): 204–17; Joshua Greene, *The Moral Self* (New York: Penguin Group,
        2011).
12.   Greene, *The Moral Self*.
13.   James G. March and Herbert A. Simon, *Organizations* (New York: John Wiley,
        1958).
14.   Joshua Greene, *Moral Tribes: Emotion, Reason and the Gap Between Us and Them*
        (London: Atlantic Books, 2013).
15.   Adapted from Philippa Foot, "The Problem of Abortion and the Doctrine of the
        Double Effect," in *Virtues and Vices* (Oxford: Basil Blackwell, 1978); Thomson,
        "Killing, Letting Die, and the Trolley Problem," 204–17; Greene, *The Moral Self*.
16.   Greene, *The Moral Self*; Fiery A. Cushman, "Crime and Punishment: Distin-
        guishing the Roles of Causal and Intentional Analyses in Moral Judgment," *Cog-
        nition* 108, no. 2 (2008): 353–80.
17.   Greene, *The Moral Self*.
18.   Greene, *The Moral Tribes*.
19.   Foot, *Virtues and Vices*.
20.   Elizabeth Kolbert, "Gospels of Giving for the New Gilded Age: Are today's
        donor classes solving problems—or creating new ones?" *The New Yorker*, Au-
        gust 20, 2018, https://www.newyorker.com/magazine/2018/08/27/gospels-of
        -giving-for-the-new-gilded-age.
21.   Jann Hoffman, "Purdue Pharma Warns That Sackler Family May Walk Away
        from Opioid Deal," *New York Times*, September 19, 2019, https://www.nytimes
        .com/2019/09/19/health/purdue-sackler-opioid-settlement.html.
22.   Anand Giridharadas, *Winners Take All: The Elite Charade of Changing the World*
        (New York: Knopf, 2018).

CHAPTER 2: CULTIVATING ACTIVE INTELLIGENCE

1.   S. Fiske and E. Borgida, eds., *Beyond Common Sense: Psychological Science in the
        Courtroom* (Hoboken, NJ: Wiley-Blackwell, 2007).
2.   Max H. Bazerman and Don Moore, *Judgment in Managerial Decision Making*, 8th
        ed. (Hoboken, NJ: John Wiley, 2013).
3.   Don A. Moore, *Perfectly Confident: How to Calibrate Your Decisions Wisely* (New
        York: Harper Business, 2020).
4.   Adapted from Bazerman and Moore, *Judgment in Managerial Decision Making*.
5.   Ibid.
6.   Ibid.; William H. Desvousges, F. Reed Johnson, Richard W. Dunford, Kevin J.
        Boyle, Sara P. Hudson, and K. Nicole Wilson, "Measuring Non-use Damages
        Using Contingent Valuation: Experimental Evaluation Accuracy," Research Tri-
        angle Inst. Monograph 92–1, 1992.
7.   Daniel Kahneman, "Comments on the Contingent Valuation Method," in *Valu-
        ing Environmental Goods: A State of the Arts Assessment of the Contingent Valuation
        Method*, ed. Ronald G. Cummings, David S. Brookshire, and William D. Schulze
        (Totowa, NJ: Roweman and Allanheld, 1986), 185–94.

8. Daniel Kahneman, Ilana Ritov, and David Schkade, "Economic Preferences or Attitude Expressions? An Analysis of Dollar Responses to Public Issues," *Journal of Risk and Uncertainty* 19, no. 1–3 (1999): 203–35.

9. Deborah A. Small, George Loewenstein, and Paul Slovic, "Sympathy and Callousness: The Impact of Deliberative Thought on Donations to Identifiable and Statistical Victims," *Organizational Behavior and Human Decision Processes* 102, no. 2 (2007): 143–53.

10. Karen Jenni and George Loewenstein, "Explaining the Identifiable Victim Effect," *Journal of Risk and Uncertainty* 14, no. 3 (1997): 235–57.

11. D. Kahneman, I. Ritov, K. E. Jacowitz, and P. Grant, "Stated Willingness to Pay for Public Goods: A Psychological Analysis," *Psychological Science* 4 (1993): 310–15.

12. P. Singer, "Affluence, and Morality," *Philosophy and Public Affairs* 1, no. 3 (1972): 229–43.

13. Nicholas Epley and Eugene M. Caruso, "Perspective Taking: Misstepping into the Others' Shoes," in *Handbook of Imagination and Mental Simulation*, ed. Keith Douglas Markman, William M. P. Klein, and Julie A. Suhr (New York: Psychology Press, 2009), 295–309.

14. Boaz Keysar, "The Illusory Transparency of Intention: Linguistic Perspective Taking in Text," *Cognitive Psychology* 26, no. 2 (1994): 165–208.

15. Moore, *Perfectly Confident*.

16. Nicholas Epley, Eugene Caruso, and Max H. Bazerman, "When Perspective Taking Increases Taking: Reactive Egoism in Social Interaction," *Journal of Personality and Social Psychology* 91, no. 5 (2007): 872–89.

17. Bazerman and Moore, *Judgment in Managerial Decision Making*.

18. Dolly Chugh, "Societal and Managerial Implications of Implicit Social Cognition: Why Milliseconds Matter," *Social Justice Research* 17, no. 2 (2004): 203–22.

19. As I write this in 2020, we have a president of the United States who seems to rely almost entirely on System 1 thinking.

20. Max H. Bazerman, Holly A. Schroth, Pri Pradhan Shah, Kristina A. Diekmann, and Ann E. Tenbrunsel, "The Inconsistent Role of Comparison Others and Procedural Justice to Hypothetical Job Descriptions: Implications for Job Acceptance Decisions," *Organizational Behavior and Human Decision Processes* 60, no. 3 (1994): 326–52.

21. Iris Bohnet, Alexandra van Geen, and Max Bazerman, "When Performance Trumps Gender Bias: Joint Versus Separate Evaluation," *Management Science* 62, no. 5 (2016): 1225–34.

22. John Rawls, *A Theory of Justice* (Cambridge, MA: Harvard University Press, 1971).

23. Joshua D. Greene, Karen Huang, and Max Bazerman, "Veil-of-Ignorance Reasoning Favors the Greater Good," *Proceedings of the National Academy of Sciences of the United States of America* (in press).

24. Claudia Goldin and Cecilia Rouse, "Orchestrating Impartiality: The Impact of Blind Auditions on Female Musicians," *American Economic Review* 90, no. 4 (2000): 715–41.

25. Linda Chang, Mina Cikara, Iris Bohnet, and Max H. Bazerman, ongoing data collection.

CHAPTER 3: MAKING WISE TRADE-OFFS

1. Lucius Caviola, Nadira Faulmuller, Jim A. C. Everett, Julian Savulescu, and Guy Kahane, "The Evaluability Bias in Charitable Giving: Saving Administration Costs or Saving Lives?" *Judgment and Decision Making* 9, no. 4 (2014): 303–15.
2. Deepak Malhotra and Max H. Bazerman, *Negotiation Genius* (New York: Bantam Books, 2007).
3. Program on Negotiation email, "Sunday Minute," September 16, 2018.
4. Tejvan Pettinger, "Benefits of Free Trade," EconomicsHelp, July 28, 2017, https://www.economicshelp.org/trade2/benefits_free_trade/.
5. Steven Kuhn, "Prisoner's Dilemma," in *The Stanford Encyclopedia of Philosophy* (Winter 2019), https://plato.stanford.edu/archives/win2019/entries/prisoner-dilemma/.
6. A. W. Tucker, "The Mathematics of Tucker: A Sampler," *The Two-Year College Mathematics Journal* 14, no. 3 (1983): 228–32.
7. Carter Racing, [A] [B] [C], Jack W. Brittain and Sim B. Sitkin, Dispute Resolution Research Centre, Northwestern University, 1988 Carter Racing Case and Teaching Notes.
8. I describe my teaching of Carter Racing in more detail in Max H. Bazerman, *The Power of Noticing* (New York: Simon & Schuster, 2014).

CHAPTER 4: DISRUPTING CORRUPTION

1. Centers for Medicaid and Medicare Services, https://www.cms.gov/Research-Statistics-Data-and-Systems/Statistics-Trends-and-Reports/NationalHealth ExpendData/downloads/highlights.pdf.
2. I served as an expert witness for the Federal Trade Commission (FTC) in multiple lawsuits, including FTC's lawsuit against Schering-Plough and Upsher-Smith. The opinions expressed here are mine and not those of the FTC.
3. James Gillespie and Max H. Bazerman, "Parasitic Integration," *Negotiation Journal* 13, no. 3 (1997): 271–82.
4. I served as an expert witness for the Federal Trade Commission (FTC) in this case against Cephalon.
5. Sana Rafiq and Max Bazerman, "Pay-for-Monopoly? An Assessment of Reverse Payment Deals by Pharmaceutical Companies," *Journal of Behavioral Economics for Policy* 3, no. 1 (2019): 37–43.
6. Josh Campbell, "America's Shredded Moral Authority," CNN, June 21, 2018, https://www.cnn.com/2018/06/20/opinions/united-states-moral-credibility -is-badly-tarnished-campbell/index.html.
7. Center for American Progress Action Fund, Progress Report, June 5, 2018, https://www.americanprogressaction.org/progress-reports/the-cost-of-corruption/.
8. Sarah Chayes, *Thieves of State: Why Corruption Threatens Global Security* (New York: W. W. Norton, 2016).
9. James Risen, *Pay Any Price: Greed, Power, and Endless War* (Boston: Houghton Mifflin Harcourt, 2014).
10. *Washington Post* Editorial Board, "Trump Slanders Khashoggi and Betrays American Values," *Washington Post*, November 20, 2018, https://www.washing tonpost.com/opinions/global-opinions/trumps-latest-statement-on-khashoggi

-was-a-betrayal-of-american-values/2018/11/20/f4efdd80-ecef-11e8-baac-2a674 e91502b_story.html?noredirect=on&utm_term=.beba86178ba1.

11. Ibid.

12. Mark Mazzetti, "Year Before Killing, Saudi Prince Told Aide He Would Use 'a Bullet' on Jamal Khashoggi," *New York Times*, February 7, 2019, https://www .nytimes.com/2019/02/07/us/politics/khashoggi-mohammed-bin-salman.html.

13. *Washington Post* Editorial Board, "Trump Slanders Khashoggi and Betrays American Values."

14. Donna Borak, "Consumer Protection Bureau Drops Payday Lender Lawsuit," January 18, 2018, CNN Business, https://money.cnn.com/2018/01/18/news/eco nomy/cfpb-lawsuit-payday-lenders/index.html.

15. *United States v. Arthur Young & Co.* (1984).

16. Max H. Bazerman, Kimberly P. Morgan, and George F. Loewenstein, "The Impossibility of Auditor Independence," *MIT Sloan Management Review* 38, no. 4 (1997); Don A. Moore, Lloyd Tanlu, and Max H. Bazerman, "Conflict of Interest and the Intrusion of Bias," *Judgment and Decision Making* 5, no. 1 (2010): 37–53.

17. Bazerman, Morgan, and Loewenstein, "The Impossibility of Auditor Independence"; Moore, Tanlu, and Bazerman, "Conflict of Interest and the Intrusion of Bias."

18. Karl Evers-Hillstrom, Raymond Arke, and Luke Robinson, "A Look at the Impact of Citizens United on Its 9th Anniversary," OpenSecrets.org, January 21, 2019, https://www.opensecrets.org/news/2019/01/citizens-united/.

19. Max H. Bazerman and Ann Tenbrunsel, *Blind Spots: Why We Fail to Do What's Right and What to Do about It* (Princeton, NJ: Princeton University Press, 2011).

20. Deborah L. Rhode, *Cheating: Ethics in Everyday Life* (Oxford: Oxford University Press, 2017).

21. Lisa L. Shu, Nina Mazar, Francesca Gino, Dan Ariely, and Max H. Bazerman, "Signing at the Beginning Makes Ethics Salient and Decreases Dishonest Self-Reports in Comparison to Signing at the End," *Proceedings of the National Academy of Sciences* 109, no. 38 (2012): 15197–200, https://doi.org/10.1073/pnas.1209746109.

22. Ibid.

23. A. Kristal, A. Whillans, M. Bazerman, F. Gino, L. Shu, N. Mazar, and D. Ariely, "Signing at the Beginning vs at the End Does Not Decrease Dishonesty: Documenting Repeated Replication Failures," *Proceedings of the National Academy of Sciences of the United States of America* 117, no. 13 (March 31, 2020).

24. https://slice.is/.

25. Max H. Bazerman, *The Power of Noticing: What the Best Leaders See* (New York: Simon & Schuster, 2014).

CHAPTER 5: ACTIVATING YOUR MORAL OBLIGATION TO NOTICE

1. Ting Zhang, Pinar O. Fletcher, Francesca Gino, and Max H. Bazerman, "Reducing Bounded Ethicality: How to Help Individuals Notice and Avoid Unethical Behavior," *Organizational Dynamics* 44, no. 4 (2015, Special Issue on Bad Behavior): 310–17.

2. Max H. Bazerman and Ann Tenbrunsel, *Blind Spots: Why We Fail to Do What's Right and What to Do about It* (Princeton, NJ: Princeton University Press, 2011).

3.   John Carreyrou, *Bad Blood: Secrets and Lies in a Silicon Valley Startup* (New York: Knopf, 2018).

4.   https://en.wikipedia.org/wiki/Theranos#cite_note-20.

5.   https://en.wikipedia.org/wiki/Theranos#cite_note-22.

6.   Jack Ewing, *Faster, Higher, Farther: The Inside Story of the Volkswagen Scandal* (New York: W. W. Norton, 2017).

7.   Ibid.

8.   Ibid.

9.   Lisa D. Ordóñez, Maurice E. Schweitzer, Adam D. Galinsky, and Max H. Bazerman, "On Good Scholarship, Goal Setting, and Scholars Gone Wild," *Academy of Management Perspectives* 23, no. 3 (2009): 82–87.

10.   Ewing, *Faster, Higher, Farther*.

11.   Ibid.

12.   James B. Stewart, "Problems at Volkswagen Start in the Boardroom," *New York Times*, September 24, 2015, https://www.nytimes.com/2015/09/25/business/international/problems-at-volkswagen-start-in-the-boardroom.html.

13.   Melissa Eddy, "Rupert Stadler, Ex-Audi Chief, Is Charged with Fraud in Diesel Scandal," *New York Times*, July 31, 2019.

14.   Bazerman and Tenbrunsel, *Blind Spots*.

15.   Ibid.

16.   Brianna Sacks, "Olympic Organizations and the FBI Knew Larry Nassar was Abusing Young Gymnasts but Didn't Do Anything for Over a Year," BuzzFeed News, July 30, 2019.

17.   Warren G. Bennis and Robert J. Thomas, *Geeks and Geezers* (Boston: HBR Press, 2002).

CHAPTER 6: REDUCING TRIBALISM AND INCREASING EQUALITY

1.   D. M. Messick, "Mortgage-Bias Complexities," *Chicago Tribune*, March 1, 1994.

2.   Joshua Greene, *Moral Tribes: Emotion, Reason and the Gap Between Us and Them* (London: Atlantic Books, 2013).

3.   Steven Pinker, *Enlightenment Now: The Case for Reason, Science, Humanism, and Progress* (New York: Viking, 2018).

4.   Anemona Hartocollis, "What's at Stake in the Harvard Lawsuit? Decades of Debate Over Race in Admissions," *New York Times*, October 13, 2018, https://www.nytimes.com/2018/10/13/us/harvard-affirmative-action-asian-students.html.

5.   Anemona Hartocollis, "Harvard Does Not Discriminate Against Asian-Americans in Admissions, Judge Rules," *New York Times*, October 1, 2019.

6.   Peter Singer, *Practical Ethics* (Cambridge: Cambridge University Press, 1979); Greene, *Moral Tribes*.

7.   Max Larkin, "Lawsuit Alleging Racial 'Balancing' at Harvard Reveals Another Preference—for Children of Alumni," October 12, 2018, WBUR, https://www.wbur.org/edify/2018/10/12/harvard-admissions-legacy-preference.

8.   This difference does not control for all other independent variables. But the difference remains large with those controls.

9.   Larkin, "Lawsuit Alleging Racial 'Balancing' at Harvard Reveals Another Preference—for Children of Alumni."

10.   Ibid.

11. Ibid.

12. Ibid.

13. Ibid.

14. Maggie Servais and Jake Gold, "Legacy Applicants Admitted to U.Va. at Nearly Two Times the Rate of Non-legacies in 2018," *Cavalier Daily*, July 2, 2018, http://www.cavalierdaily.com/article/2018/07/legacy-applicants-admitted-to-at-nearly-two-times-the-rate-of-non-legacies-in-2018.

15. E. O. Wilson, *Sociobiology: The New Synthesis* (Cambridge, MA: Harvard University Press, 1975).

16. Greene, *Moral Tribes*.

17. Gerd Gigerenzer and Reinhard Selten, eds., *Bounded Rationality: The Adaptive Toolbox* (Cambridge, MA: MIT Press, 2001); Gerd Gigerenzer, Peter M. Todd, and the ABC Research Group, *Simple Heuristics That Make Us Smart* (Oxford: Oxford University Press, 1999).

18. Laurie R. Santos and Alexandra G. Rosati, "The Evolutionary Roots of Human Decision Making," *Annual Review of Psychology* 3 (2015): 321–47.

19. Greene, *Moral Tribes*.

20. Wilson, *Sociobiology*; Peter Singer, *The Expanding Circle* (Princeton, NJ: Princeton University Press, 1981).

21. Anthony Greenwald and Mahzarin Banaji, *Blindspot: Hidden Biases of Good People* (New York: Delacorte Press, 2013).

22. Amy Wu, "Scholar Spotlight: Dolly Chugh Discusses Her New Book," Ethical Systems, October 30, 2018, https://www.ethicalsystems.org/content/scholar-spotlight-dolly-chugh-discusses-her-new-book.

23. Singer, *Practical Ethics*.

24. Ibid.

25. Jeremy Bentham, *Introduction to the Principles of Morals and Legislation* (1789).

CHAPTER 7: IDENTIFYING AND ELIMINATING WASTE

1. Tom Kemeny and Taner Osman, "The Wider Impacts of High-Technology Employment: Evidence from U.S. Cities," Working Paper, London School of Economics and Political Science, September 16, 2017, http://www.lse.ac.uk/International-Inequalities/Assets/Documents/Working-Papers/Working-Paper-16-The-Wider-Impacts-of-High-Technology-Employment-Evidence-from-U.S.-cities-Tom-Kemeny-and-Taner-Osman.pdf.

2. Dennis Green, "The Professor Who Predicted Amazon Would Buy Whole Foods Says Only 2 Cities Have a Shot at HQ2," *Business Insider*, February 12, 2018, https://www.recode.net/2018/11/9/18077342/amazon-hq2-headquarters-jeff-bezos-dc-ny-virginia-long-island-kara-swisher-scott-galloway.

3. Lauren Feiner, "Amazon Says It Will Not Build a Headquarters in New York," CNBC, February 15, 2019, https://www.cnbc.com/2019/02/14/amazon-says-it-will-not-build-a-headquarters-in-new-york-after-mounting-opposition-reuters-reports.html.

4. Derek Thompson, "Amazon's HQ2 Spectacle Isn't Just Shameful—It Should be Illegal," *Atlantic*, November 12, 2018, https://www.theatlantic.com/ideas/archive/2018/11/amazons-hq2-spectacle-should-be-illegal/575539/.

5. Ed Shanahan, "Amazon Grows in New York, Reviving Debate Over Abandoned Queens Project," *New York Times*, December 6, 2019, https://www.nytimes .com/2019/12/06/nyregion/amazon-hudson-yards.html.

6. Alexander K. Gold, Austin J. Drukker, and Ted Gayer, "Why the Federal Government Should Stop Spending Billions on Private Sports Stadiums," Brookings Institution, September 8, 2016, https://www.brookings.edu/research/why-the -federal-government-should-stop-spending-billions-on-private-sports-stadiums/.

7. Ibid.

8. Ibid.

9. Max H. Bazerman, Jonathan Baron, and Katherine Shonk, *You Can't Enlarge the Pie: Six Barriers to Effective Government* (New York: Basic Books, 2001).

10. Garrett Hardin, "The Tragedy of the Commons," *Science* 162 (1968): 1243–48.

11. Max H. Bazerman and William F. Samuelson, "I Won the Auction but Don't Want the Prize," *Journal of Conflict Resolution* 27 (1983): 618–34.

12. Ibid.

13. Amy Liu, "Landing HQ2 Isn't the Right Way for a City to Create Jobs. Here's What Works Instead," Brookings Institution, August 7, 2018, https://www .brookings.edu/blog/the-avenue/2018/08/07/landing-amazon-hq2-isnt-the -right-way-for-a-city-to-create-jobs-heres-what-works-instead/.

14. Harish, "Animals We Use and Abuse for Food We Do Not Eat," Counting Animals website, March 27, 2013, http://www.countinganimals.com/animals-we -use-and-abuse-for-food-we-do-not-eat/.

15. A. Leonard, *The Story of Stuff*, http://www.thestoryofstuff.com.

16. F. Shahidi and J. R. Botta, "Seafoods: Chemistry, Processing Technology and Quality," Springer Science & Business Media, 2012.

17. Maria Martinez Romero, "Tristam [*sic*] Stuart Uncovers the Global Food Waste Scandal," *Morningside Post*, March 25, 2017, https://morningsidepost.com /articles/2017/9/9/tristam-stuart-uncovers-the-global-food-waste-scandal.

18. Harish, "Animals We Use and Abuse for Food We Do Not Eat."

19. Tim Searchinger, Richard Waite, Craig Hanson, Janet Ranganathan, World Resources Institute, "World Resources Report: Creating a Sustainable Food Future," July 2019, https://www.wri.org/our-work/project/world-resources-report /world-resources-report-creating-sustainable-food-future.

20. "Plant-Based Food Growing at 20 Percent, Data Shows," *FSR*, July 30, 2018, https://www.foodnewsfeed.com/content/plant-based-foods-growing-20-per cent-data-shows.

21. About, Glasswall Syndicate, https://glasswallsyndicate.org/ (accessed October 28, 2019).

22. Beth Kowitt, "Tyson Foods Has Invested in a Startup That Aims to Eradicate Meat from Live Animals," *Fortune*, January 29, 2018, http://fortune.com/2018 /01/29/tyson-memphis-meats-investment/.

23. https://phys.org/news/2011–04-energy_1.html.

24. Mike Snider, "Dozens of Fake Charities Scammed Donations for Veterans Then Pocketed the Cash: FTC," *USA Today*, July 19, 2018, https://www.usatoday.com /story/money/business/2018/07/19/charity-call-help-vets-scam-so-were-many -others-ftc/797959002/.

25. Ibid.

26. GrantSpace, "How Many Nonprofit Organizations Are There in the United States?" https://grantspace.org/resources/knowledge-base/number-of-nonprofits-in-the-u-s/ (accessed October 28, 2019).

27. Janet Greenlee and Teresa Gordon, "The Impact of Professional Solicitors on Fundraising in Charitable Organizations," *Nonprofit & Voluntary Sector Quarterly*, September 1998.

28. Bazerman, Baron, and Shonk, *You Can't Enlarge the Pie*.

29. Sacha Pfeiffer, "Does Boston Have Too Many Nonprofits? Some Say Yes," *Boston Globe*, July 4, 2016, https://www.bostonglobe.com/business/2016/07/04/does-boston-have-too-many-nonprofits-some-say-yes/XMnV259wjXdugZqrOl3CvI/story.html.

CHAPTER 8: ALLOCATING YOUR MOST PRECIOUS ASSET—YOUR TIME

1. Adapted from Amos Tversky and Daniel Kahneman, "The Framing of Decisions and the Psychology of Choice," *Science* 211 (1981): 453–58; Max H. Bazerman and Don Moore, *Judgment in Managerial Decision Making*, 7th ed. (New York: Wiley, 2009).

2. Readers may be thinking about the cost of gas and wear and tear on the car, but you will see that these remain constant across the two questions.

3. Adapted from Tversky and Kahneman, "The Framing of Decisions and the Psychology of Choice."

4. Cassie Mogilner, Ashley Whillans, and Michael I. Norton, "Time, Money, and Subjective Well-being," *Handbook of Well-Being* (Salt Lake City, UT: DEF, 2018). Retrieved from nobascholar.com.

5. Ibid.

6. Ashley Whillans, *A Happier Time* (Cambridge, MA: Harvard Business School Press, 2020).

7. Ibid.

8. David Ricardo, *On the Principles of Political Economy and Taxation* (Mineola, NY: Dover, 2004). Originally published in 1817.

9. Mary Allen, "How a Cardiologist Is Using Meat to Save More Lives," Good Food Institute, August 10, 2018, https://www.gfi.org/how-a-cardiologist-is-using-meat-to-save.

10. Ibid.

11. Ben Todd, "Your Career Can Help Solve the World's Most Pressing Problems," 80,000 Hours, October 2019, https://80000hours.org/key-ideas/#further-reading-5.

12. Scott Alexander, "Efficient Charity: Do Unto Others," Effective Altruism, September 3, 2013, https://www.effectivealtruism.org/articles/efficient-charity-do-unto-others/.

13. Linda Babcock, Maria Recalde, Lisa Verterlund, and Laurie Weingart, "Gender Differences in Accepting and Receiving Requests for Tasks with Low Promotability," *American Economic Review* 107 (2017): 714–47.

CHAPTER 9: GETTING THE MOST BANG FOR YOUR PHILANTHROPIC BUCK

1. Scott Simon, "When Disaster Relief Brings Anything but Relief," CBS News, September 3, 2017, https://www.cbsnews.com/news/best-intentions-when-disaster-relief-brings-anything-but-relief/.

2. Ibid.

3. Ibid.

4. Elizabeth Williamson, "A Lesson of Sandy Hook: 'Err on the Side of the Victims,'" *New York Times*, May 25, 2019, https://www.nytimes.com/2019/05/25/us/politics/sandy-hook-money.html.

5. Simon, "When Disaster Relief Brings Anything but Relief."

6. C-SPAN, "Charity Navigator," https://www.c-span.org/organization/?112167/Charity-Navigator (accessed October 28, 2019).

7. Lisa D. Ordóñez, Maurice E. Schweitzer, Adam D. Galinsky, and Max H. Bazerman, "Goals Gone Wild: The Systematic Side Effects of Over-Prescribing Goal Setting," *Academy of Management Perspectives* 23 (2009): 6–16.

8. "Introduction to Effective Altruism," Effective Altruism, June 22, 2016, https://www.effectivealtruism.org/articles/introduction-to-effective-altruism/.

9. William MacAskill, *Doing Good Better: How Effective Altruism Can Help You Help Others, Do Work That Matters, and Make Smarter Choices about Giving Back* (New York: Avery, 2016).

10. See, for example, Sara Cappe, "Why Emotional Connections Drive Donations: Lessons from Academic Literature," Maru/Matchbox, January 18, 2018, https://marumatchbox.com/why-emotional-connections-drive-donating-lessons-from-the-academic-literature/.

11. Max H. Bazerman, "Raiffa Transformed the Field of Negotiation—and Me," *Negotiation and Conflict Management Research* 11 (2018): 259–61.

12. John Rawls, *A Theory of Justice* (Cambridge, MA: Harvard University Press, 1971).

CHAPTER 10: MULTIPLYING VALUE CREATION THROUGH OTHERS

1. Betsey Stevenson and Justin Wolfers, "Subjective Well-Being and Income: Is There Any Evidence of Satiation?" *American Economic Review, Papers and Proceedings* 101 (May 2013): 598–604.

2. William MacAskill, *Doing Good Better: How Effective Altruism Can Help You Help Others, Do Work That Matters, and Make Smarter Choices about Giving Back* (New York: Avery, 2016).

3. Ibid.

4. There was a small effect for the best-performing students.

5. MacAskill, *Doing Good Better*.

6. Toby Ord, "How Many Lives Can You Save? Taking Charity Seriously," March 25, 2013, https://www.youtube.com/watch?v=iGCVRA7T7FE&feature=youtu.be.

7. D.C. Taylor-Robinson, N. Maayan, S. Donegan, M. Chaplin, and P. Garner, "Deworming School Children in Low and Middle Income Countries," Cochrane, September 11, 2019, https://www.cochrane.org/CD000371/INFECTN_deworming-school-children-low-and-middle-income-countries.

8. Dean T. Jamison, Joel G. Breman, Anthony R. Measham, George Alleyne, Mariam Claeson, David B. Evans, Prabhat Jha, Anne Mills, and Philip Musgrove, *Disease Control Priorities in Developing Countries*, 2nd ed. (New York: Oxford University Press and the World Bank, 2006). See also: https://docs.google.com/spreadsheets/d/1OvRumP4GAx5GZ2IYJpUE3CPMG1e9r4g8kWugKmOPFHE/edit#gid=1.

9. R. Fisher, *Statistical Methods for Research Workers*, 13th ed. (Edinburgh: Oliver & Boyd, 1963).

10. Michael Luca and Max H. Bazerman, *The Power of Experiments* (Cambridge, MA: MIT Press, 2020).

11. Ibid.

12. Ibid.

13. Barry Schwartz, "Why Not Nudge? A Review of Cass Sunstein's Why Nudge," Psych Report, April 17, 2014, http://thepsychreport.com/essays-discussion/nudge -review-cass-sunsteins-why-nudge/.

14. Luca and Bazerman, *The Power of Experiments*.

15. Peter Singer, *The Most You Can Do* (New Haven, CT: Yale University Press, 2015).

16. Eric J. Johnson and Daniel G. Goldstein, "Do Defaults Save Lives?" Science 302 (2003): 1338–39.

17. There is an active debate in the literature over whether opt-out or forcing people to choose is the better strategy. For our purposes, I am simply highlighting the comparison between opt-in and opt-out.

18. Richard Thaler and Cass Sunstein, *Nudge: Improving Decisions about Health, Wealth, and Happiness* (New Haven, CT: Yale University Press, 2008).

19. Shlomo Benartzi, John Beshears, Katherine L. Milkman, Cass Sunstein, Richard H. Thaler, Maya Shankar, Will Tucker, William J. Congdon, and Steven Galing, "Should Governments Invest More in Nudging?" *Psychological Science* 28 (2017): 1041–55.

20. Howard Raiffa, *The Art and Science of Negotiation* (Cambridge, MA: Belknap, 1982); David A. Lax and James K. Sebenius, *The Manager as Negotiator: Bargaining for Cooperation and Competitive Gain* (New York: Free Press, 1986); Deepak Malhotra and Max H. Bazerman, *Negotiation Genius: How to Overcome Obstacles and Achieve Brilliant Results at the Bargaining Table and Beyond* (New York: Bantam, 2007).

21. Dolly Chugh, *The Person You Mean to Be: How Good People Fight Bias* (New York: Harper Business, 2018).

22. Elizabeth Dunn and Michael Norton, *Happy Money: The Science of Happier Spending* (New York: Simon & Schuster, 2014).

23. Steven Pinker. *Enlightenment Now: The Case for Reason, Science, Humanism, and Progress* (New York: Penguin, 2019).

CHAPTER 11: MAXIMUM SUSTAINABLE GOODNESS

1. Edward S. Russell, "Some Theoretical Considerations on the 'Overfishing' Problem," *ICES Journal of Marine Science* 6 (1931): 3–20; Michael Graham, "Modern Theory of Exploiting a Fishery, and Application to North Sea Trawling," *ICES Journal of Marine Science* 10 (1935): 264–74.

2. Ray Hilborn and Ulrike Hilborn, *Overfishing: What Everyone Needs to Know* (Oxford: Oxford University Press, 2012).

3. "U.N. Report Urges Plant-Based Diets to Combat Climate Change," Animal Equality, August 16, 2019, https://animalequality.org/blog/2019/08/16/un-report -urges-plant-based-diets-to-combat-climate-change/.

4. Behavioral Insights Interview with Max H. Bazerman—EAGxBoston 2018," April 21, 2018, https://www.youtube.com/watch?v=B8TOz25ctGw.

5.   Dan Harris, *10% Happier: How I Tamed the Voice in My Head, Reduced Stress Without Losing My Edge, and Found Self-Help That Actually Works—A True Story* (New York: HarperCollins, 2014).

6.   Peter Singer, *The Most Good You Can Do* (New Haven, CT: Yale University Press, 2015).

7.   Tobias Leenaert, *How to Create a Vegan World* (New York: Lantern Books, 2017).

8.   https://mises.org/wire/altruism-really-virtue.

9.   Martin Luther King Jr., *Strength to Love* (Minneapolis: Fortress Press, 2010).

INDEX

ABOUT THE AUTHOR

Max H. Bazerman is Jesse Isidor Straus Professor of Business Administration at the Harvard Business School. *Better, Not Perfect* is Max's eleventh book. His books include *The Power of Experiments* (with Michael Luca), *The Power of Noticing*, *Judgment in Managerial Decision Making* (with Don Moore), and *Blind Spots* (with Ann Tenbrunsel).

Max received an honorary doctorate from the University of London, the Life Achievement Award from the Aspen Institute's Business and Society Program, the Distinguished Educator Award from the Academy of Management, the Academy of Management Career Award for Scholarly Contributions to Management, and the Lifetime Achievement Award from the Organizational Behavior Division of the Academy of Management. In addition, Max was named as one of Ethisphere's 100 Most Influential People in Business Ethics and as one of Daily Kos's Heroes for going public about how the Bush administration corrupted the RICO Tobacco trial.

Max's consulting, teaching, and lecturing includes work in thirty countries.